TALES OUT OF CONGRESS

TALES OUT OF

Congress

By Stephen M. Young
United States Senator from Ohio

J.B. LIPPINCOTT COMPANY

Philadelphia and New York

TALES OUT OF CONGRESS

ACKNOWLEDGMENTS

The author would like to thank particularly Mr. Paul Kresh for his unflagging editorial and literary help and support over the many months it took to compile, assemble and organize the material for this volume.

I would also like to express my gratitude to Mr. Herbert Jolovitz of Canton, Ohio, my administrative assistant, for his help, suggestions, research and careful scrutiny of these pages in advance of publication, in the midst of the longest Congressional session in American history.

CHAPTER 1

🔖 *YOUNG TO RUN, TRUMAN PREDICTS: That was the headline my wife Rachel Bell held up for me to see when I woke up on the morning of September 14, 1963, in our suite at the Sheraton-Cleveland in Ohio's largest city. I had gone out to greet former President Truman at Cleveland-Hopkins Airport the night before, and his announcement that I was to run again was as much news to me as to the people of Ohio.*

I hadn't yet made up my own mind. At the age of seventy-four, after serving four terms as Ohio's Representative-at-large and five-sixths of my first term as a United States Senator, I was not quite so sure as Mr. Truman that I was eager for another six years in the Senate. I still had all my faculties unimpaired, as they say in the insurance advertisements. I felt young and healthy—at least I did until at the airport I stepped up to shake hands with our former President. At seventy-nine he seemed to be about twice as young and healthy as I felt. Wearing a light blue suit with a pearl gray hat set on his head at a jaunty angle, he exuded energy and confidence. As we were shaking hands a reporter asked him if he thought I would really run for the Senate again.

"Why, I wouldn't have come all this way if I didn't think so. I hope I haven't beaten him to the punch by saying it, but do you want to put up five cents to bet he won't?'"

Frankly, I felt I had over the years acquired skill and experience in the science of government. I have frequently

9

said that being a Senator is just a job like any other job but a very hard one. Sometimes I thought, "Why not retire at the end of this term and practice law in Cleveland and Washington; why work so hard and such long hours six days a week—sometimes seven?" A hard question to answer.

The reason Mr. Truman and I were in Cleveland at all, along with six other Senators, including several from such far-flung outposts as Hawaii and Alaska, was to celebrate a kind of political birthday, which happens to you if you stay in politics long enough and persuade enough of your fellow citizens to mark a cross or pull the right lever on a sufficient number of election days. They call this sort of tribute an "Appreciation Day" and, as I had been in the political arena since I first ran for the Ohio General Assembly in 1912, apparently I qualified. At least some of my good friends thought so.

I guess the real test for an Appreciation Day is to see if the public official can survive the agenda. It's a sort of political equivalent of the old Spartan custom of placing newborn babies out on a mountain overnight to eliminate the weaklings. If you live through an Appreciation Day, they sometimes let you run again, and meanwhile, at one hundred dollars a plate, they have managed to raise some of the funds you will need in order to do so.

My personal Appreciation Day dawned bright and sunny. The man on the radio told me it was 37 degrees outside, but it was to get a lot warmer than that before the day was over, and so was I. I didn't have to get up quite so early as I might have since Mr. Truman was busy preparing his address for a dinner that evening and passed up his usual morning walk in order to work on it. The hotel had installed Rachel and me in a handsome suite, a far cry from the kind of single room I had squeezed myself into in my early days as a struggling lawyer. I wonder what I would have made then of the spacious rooms and sumptuous furnishings, the satin curtains

10

and deep, luxurious sofas! There was one room all paneled in wood and decorated with antiques from the Revolutionary War, not to mention letters from people like former President Eisenhower thanking the management for a lovely stay, suitably framed and staring at you from the high-priced paneling. I started to inspect this intriguing correspondence, but there was no time for a proper study. The day's events were under way.

At 9:30 there was a press conference for Mr. Truman in the Whitehall Room. He told reporters he didn't care what candidate the Republicans ran, "We'll lick 'em anyway." He said he would be in Atlantic City as a Missouri delegate to the 1964 Democratic Convention. "How could they run a convention without me there raising hell?" was the way he put it. He told reporters President Kennedy's civil rights bill, which had been keeping us Senators in Washington the entire summer, was a copy of one he himself had sent to Congress in 1948. He was to say a lot more on this subject before the day was over, not all of it calculated to appeal to the liberal mind.

After the press conference Mr. Truman invited newspapermen back to his suite at the hotel for a concert, since the subject of his piano-playing had come up. He played Paderewski's Minuet for them to a violin accompaniment by Mr. Walter J. Touhey, president of the Chesapeake and Ohio Railroad.

By the time President Truman had issued enough snappy replies to questions to satisfy the slowest-writing reporters in the Whitehall Room, guests were beginning to pour into the lobby of the Sheraton-Cleveland for the day's activities. Among them were Senators Alan Bible of Nevada, E. L. (Bob) Bartlett of Alaska, Daniel K. Inouye of Hawaii and Frank Moss of Utah. I also was conscious of others who were not there, especially my close personal friend, Senator Clair Engle of California, who was gravely ill following brain surgery. Clair, one of our great Senators with a fine political future, had apparently suffered an injury while boxing or playing football in his college days. My fellow Senator from Ohio, Frank J. Lausche, had been expected to attend but found it difficult to leave Washington. Others who couldn't make it were Senators Pat McNamara of Michigan, Gale McGee of Wyoming and Edward (Ted) Kennedy of Massachusetts. Some were attending an interparliamentary conference in Belgrade.

As I came down to the lobby I saw my administrative assistant, Herb Jolovitz, trying to get attention on a house telephone. He looked as though he were gasping for air as various members of our team, including a banquet committee, crowded around him. I felt like someone who has just been shown the engine room of a ship he thought up to then was sailing along smoothly without anyone having to stoke the boilers to keep it moving. It took the work of many hands to make this one day run smoothly, and none of the stokers would be able to stop worrying or working until it was all over—many, many hours later.

At noon we all filed into the Whitehall Room once more for another session of interviews. Techniques for getting news have certainly changed since the days when a reporter with a notebook seemed all that was necessary to find out what a man had to say about anything. You walk into one of these big halls and what with the lights, the cameras, the technicians and the general hullabaloo you would think you had wandered by mistake onto a set where they were filming "Cleopatra." They placed us Senators at a long table and turned on the bright lights. One of the things that particularly made me uneasy was the line-up of tape recorders from the various radio stations, sitting there turning and turning in their little colored plastic cases like mechanical correspondents from news syndicates in the Twilight Zone. Former Ohio State Senator Howard M. Metzenbaum, my

12

campaign manager in 1958 and chairman for the day's events, started the conference going. Most of the questions fired at my fellow Senators concerned the nuclear test ban treaty, which was before the Senate for ratification. Senators Bartlett and Inouye and I were for it, while Bible said he was uncommitted but "leaning toward approval," and Moss said, "I am *inclined* to support it." Senator Bartlett informed us that there was no use thinking of Alaska as some savage outpost exempt from fall-out dangers. He told the press that the Eskimos of Alaska eat a great deal of caribou meat and that caribou in turn subsist on lichen. Recent tests had shown that the lichen were absorbing a large amount of fall-out from the Alaskan air. The Senators made some unsparing remarks about the "radical right," John Birchers and others in our Western states and agreed that the President of South Vietnam ought to put his own political house in order, or else. The inevitable question was asked of me, "When do you plan to announce your candidacy?" I explained that my wife didn't want me to run, but my daughter did. I said I was not as old as I hoped to be, but then again I was not as young as I used to be and I was thinking the whole thing over.

The rest of the conference was devoted to the question of whether it would be possible to invoke cloture to hasten civil rights legislation, which was keeping us all in Washington at a time we had hoped to be in our own states. Most of the Senators present were against cloture. They are against shutting off debate in the Senate. I am, too, but I feel, especially in the cause of civil rights, that cloture must be invoked after full and fair debates.

A man from the local Channel 5 television station asked me for an interview on a program called "Man in the News." He asked me how I felt about getting all this attention. I said, "I guess I ought to say I feel very humble, but I will do my best to fight it." I also said I couldn't consider this Appreciation Day a bona fide political occasion since there were a lot

13

of Republicans taking part. I remarked that I would not be in the Senate except that many Republicans had always supported me. When the interviewer asked me about my health, I assured him that I had not missed a single day at work due to illness in more than four and a half years, that I am in my office in the Senate from 8:00 a.m. to 7:00 p.m. six days a week, and that if I failed to run again it wouldn't be because I wasn't physically up to it.

Indeed, I emerged from the Whitehall Room having talked myself into a state of fitness that was thoroughly exhilarating, until I encountered Mr. Truman again. When it comes to vitality there aren't many people of any age in this country who can compete with him. We were conducted through corridors, up elevators and into various suites where a series of luncheons for special groups, such as labor unions, were under way. Wherever we went the diners would rise to their feet to cheer our former President, and I stood there basking in reflected glory.

Mr. Truman will do anything at all for the Democratic party. It is a religion with him. He was stopped in the hall time after time by two or three obscure Democrats he might have brushed off with complete impunity, but no matter what they asked him, whether it was to take time out to pose with them for a photograph for a local newspaper, to autograph a picture, or just to pass the time of day, he did so. He always agreed with the utmost courtesy and total lack of condescension. Harry never plays the game of "give them hell" with the little man. His heavy ammunition is reserved for the big, dangerous targets he thinks deserve it.

At lunch, Mr. Truman and I were joined by Cleveland's Mayor Ralph S. Locher, several of the visiting Senators and a number of Congressmen. Mr. Truman was in tremendously good form. He told jokes with stinging political points which I was confident I would remember when I came to write this chapter; somehow they escape me now. He talked with en-

14

thusiasm of the new, ambitious library he had helped to found in his home town of Independence. I asked him about his hotel accommodations. He said, "I got a little hole up there almost as good as yours." (The spacious Greenbriar Suite.) About his wife Bess he commented, "A fellow needs a wife like Bess. He needs one person in this world who will talk to him frankly." He dominated the table talk, but nobody minded. Harry Truman talks a lot but he is never dull.

What with the special guards who were escorting Mr. Truman everywhere, people on all sides addressing him as "Mr. President," and the air of excitement and reverence he generated wherever he made his brisk way, I began to believe before the day was over that he *still* was the President. I had to remind myself every once in a while that the White House was occupied by another, larger family.

After lunch I hurried up to my suite in the hope of getting to read that intriguing correspondence between Mr. Eisenhower and the Sheraton Hotel people. Not a chance! The phone never stopped ringing. Assistants and well-wishers never stopped bursting in to shake hands or take up a problem—sometimes both at once. Since I have always detested politicians who spurn the friendship of those who elect them and try to surround themselves with an aura of privacy like certain temperamental movie actors, I took all the calls and answered all the questions. Before Rachel and I knew it, it was two o'clock and time to leave for a reception and cocktail party at the home of my campaign manager in Shaker Heights.

I don't know what the passers-by made of the line-up of limousines with flags flying which filled one whole side of Public Square in front of the Sheraton-Cleveland. One might easily have gotten the impression that Cleveland was being visited by at least six foreign heads of state, or that the city had been captured, perhaps, by some unemployed dictator like Trujillo. Rachel and I felt a little awed ourselves as the

15

driver of our car, who happened to be a member of the Young Republican Club, opened the door with a flourish to which we were unaccustomed. In truth, we are not in the habit of being driven about in black limousines. It might be said almost axiomatically that where there is pomp in the nation's capital you won't be likely to find the Youngs.

Driving through Cleveland to Howard Metzenbaum's house in Shaker Heights was like cutting through a cross-section of every stratum of economic and ethnic life. A few years ago there was severe unemployment in the city as the result of the sudden automation of many industrial plants. That September, however, employment was high again. Even so, there were many blighted areas. Passing through downtown Cleveland I got the feeling that one of these days it might turn into a ghost city. The trend, as in so many metropolitan communities, is out to the suburbs. The big department stores are holding their own, but many of the little shops are closing down. On this Saturday afternoon Euclid Avenue was still thronged with shoppers. But business is not what it used to be. More and more people are making their purchases in the shopping centers that have sprung up all over suburban America. Yet the city planners have high hopes that the rehabilitation of the lake front and the housing projects of downtown Cleveland will entice people back to the city. I hope they are right.

As we passed through the seedier areas on the periphery of the city I wondered why it is that grimy black tenements and rundown stores, stretches of streets without character or civic pride or focus, should blight our American landscape at all in a time of so much prosperity and enterprise. The hard light of the sun brought the sad look of these neighborhoods to our attention with a terrifying and accusing clarity. A conscientious Senator likes to feel that he has over the years spoken and voted for measures to improve the lot of his fellow Americans; that through the legislation progres-

16

sives have supported we have kept this country's wealth from accumulating dangerously in the hands of the few and have insured a decent life for a larger number of Americans than ever before. Driving through the rundown parts of Cleveland I was reawakened to the truth of how far we still have to go. Many times it has struck me how much remains to be done in the war against poverty in the United States; that it is wrong to deny worthy and industrious men and women gainful employment. Not only wrong but a disgrace. Every family needs and should have a breadwinner.

Meanwhile, escorted by the police with sirens blaring, our line of cars seemed to have a mesmeric effect on the people in the streets, who would suddenly stand stock-still to stare at this strange and unlikely procession disrupting the quiet afternoon.

To enter the incorporated community of Shaker Heights after a trip like that is quite a jolt. Not only is Shaker Heights the richest community in the country now—they tell me it is even richer than Beverly Hills—but it remains among the most beautiful. The lawns are greener, the trees taller, the houses statelier and more elegant than anywhere else in Ohio. Howard's home holds its own very well—considering that some of his income derives from the car rental company that calls itself "only Number Two."

I had been in the tasteful rooms and beautiful garden of that house often before. On this day Howard and his wife Shirley had outdone themselves. Mr. Truman was soon ensconced in a chair under a tree where he was kept busy most of the afternoon autographing every manner of document, including several history books in which his picture appears. The garden was thronged with influential local men and women. There were government officials, judges, authors, journalists, political moguls. While waiting at the bar for a drink, I counted more than ten Republicans stepping up for theirs. The garden is enormous and the swimming pool has a printed list of rules just like a municipal establishment—which should give you an idea of its vast size.

My old friend Judge Samuel Silbert asked how I was getting along and what I thought I was doing in this place. "I've come here," I explained, "to see how the poor Democrats live."

Pretty soon the entire area was filled. It was impossible to suppress a thrill of pride that all these celebrations were in the interest of sending me back to the Senate.

Along about four o'clock Mr. Truman indicated that he would like to leave soon so that we could rest up before the big dinner that evening. Word had come, however, that Leonard Bernstein, who was conducting a series of concerts in town, was on his way over to the party. Mr. Truman lingered for a while. Finally, he said he must go. As our limousine was about to start off, with Rachel and me in the back seat next to Mr. Truman, another limousine arrived, conveying Mr. Bernstein. The idol of the music-loving public was instantly surrounded by a crush of admirers, including my two granddaughters, Virginia and Caroline. They had been pleased to meet Mr. Truman earlier, but they just about swooned over Mr. Bernstein. Bernstein was able to free himself long enough to come over to our car and shake hands with us. Mr. Truman greeted him warmly, as one musician, I guess, to another. A minute later, as we were driving back toward Cleveland, he turned to my wife and said, "That musician feller should have got here on time if he wanted to meet me."

It was good to get back to the hotel for a brief rest, but it seemed only a few minutes later that we were on our way to another cocktail party, a pre-dinner reception before the main event.

At 7:30 we all went into the grand ballroom. The huge room, which had only recently been rebuilt and redecorated, was a patriotic symphony in red, white and blue. A gigantic

18

backcloth of blue stars on a black ground hung above the dais. There was one white star among the blue, the symbolism of which was never made quite clear to me. There were gigantic photographs of Kennedy, Johnson, Truman and myself. Two more Senators—Warren Magnuson of Washington and Howard Cannon of Nevada—were among those who filed on to the dais. The orchestra played "Missouri Waltz" for Mr. Truman and "Lili Marlene" for me. Mike Douglas, one of the local TV celebrities, sang the national anthem and the Reverend Clarence E. Elwell, Auxiliary Bishop of Cleveland, gave the invocation. I guess I will never be sophisticated enough not to get a lump in my throat at such a time. Nowadays, when they can blow your snapshot up to any size they please, and celebrities of all kinds are created overnight —electronically, as it were—it is a good idea to keep reminding yourself that actually you are only life-size, with all the usual human failings. Still, it is pretty hard to open a dinner menu, read your own life story in capsule form on the opening page and not be a little impressed, if only secretly. I was happy to learn from the program that I am "a leader of men . . . a legislator whose breadth of Congressional experience has extended through the terms of four Presidents . . . a humanitarian regarded as a friend by the highest officials of the nation and by those of humble origin who most need his aid." My head began to swell just a little as I dipped into my "Fruit of Seasons Lakes with Remouillade Sauce"—translation: seafood cocktail—and didn't begin to go down to normal size until I was through the "Roasted Sliced Prime Tenderloin of Beef with Sauce Champignon," and the "Senatorial Bombe" for dessert.

After dinner, Howard, who was toastmaster, pointed out that back in 1958, when everyone was expecting Bricker and not me to be elected Ohio's Senator, "I don't think we could have put this many people in a hall if we paid them two dollars apiece." Mayor Ralph S. Locher, in welcoming the guests, said all he was hoping for was "a seat in the Senate gallery to view your swearing in on January 3, 1965." Then Howard began introducing the guests, which took quite a while. There was William Coleman, chairman of the Democratic party of Ohio; Congressman Charles Vanik, five-term Congressman from the Twenty-first District and a long-time friend; Congressman Michael Feighan from the Twentieth District, recently appointed chairman of the House of Representatives Immigration Subcommittee of the Judiciary Committee; Stephen Smith, President Kennedy's brother-in-law and Democratic National Committee executive; Charlie Carr, majority leader of the Cleveland City Council; Secretary of Health, Education and Welfare Anthony Celebrezze; the six visiting Senators; Dr. Benjamin Spock, the child care authority (I think he got the biggest hand of the evening); Mayor Edward Erickson of Akron. . . . The list went on. By this time former Governor Mike DiSalle had arrived, to be greeted with applause.

There was one young man who was never introduced. I felt badly about that because I know that without him the day's events could not have gone as well as they did. He was my administrative assistant, Herb Jolovitz, who, along with Howard Metzenbaum's Cleveland law partner, Harold Stern, had been working around the clock for weeks to make this day a success.

When the introductions were over, Senator Bible praised me as a man who "says what he thinks in decisive and vigorous words and easily understood terms." My ears started to turn pink and my head began swelling again. Senator Bartlett said,

"I do not know whether this is in the nature of a kickoff dinner or whether later in the evening Steve Young is going to get up and say that he isn't going to run again. My words would have been the same in either case. He and President Truman have much in common. Both are cou-

20

rageous, both are vital, both are great actors, both are the greatest letter writers of all time."

Both Senators Bible and Bartlett were referring to my brief and tart responses to constituents' insulting letters.

Senator Cannon spoke of my letters, too. "When a citizen receives a great letter from Steve," he said, "he knows that it was personally written by him in his own style and candor and bears his own brand, to borrow a Western term."

Senator Moss added more kind words and Senator Inouye said he had come all the way from Hawaii, hoping that "in my small and humble way we may be able to urge Steve Young to seek re-election."

The remarkable part about the speeches that evening by these Senators was not their kind references to me—it was, after all, that sort of occasion—but the fact that each of them managed to keep a promise to trim his remarks down to 120 seconds. That certainly constituted a sort of oratorical landmark.

After some telegrams had been read from other Senators, including Hubert Humphrey, Ted Kennedy, Gene McCarthy and others, Senator Magnuson, on whom no time limit had been placed, got up and in his speech accorded me the highest praise imaginable—"He can spot a phony," Senator Magnuson said, "a thousand miles away."

John Bailey, the chairman of the Democratic National Committee, had more words of praise. Ray T. Miller, the Democratic leader in Cleveland, recalled the days when we had first met while I was serving my second term as an Ohio legislator: "Steve went to the Mexican Border territory in the line company of the Cleveland Grays. He worked as a member of the military machine-gun unit. We were both on the Mexican Border and then I saw Steve Young in action as a soldier. While he was a soldier he was running for Congress in Cleveland. He has never avoided a contest."

Dorothy Fuldheim, noted news analyst and television commentator, pointed out that in 1958 only one newspaper in the entire state of Ohio had supported me for election.

Tony Celebrezze observed that the Republicans had their day last week "at five dollars a throw" when Senator Barry Goldwater had spoken in Cleveland. "I think it balanced out," Celebrezze continued. "Five dollars for Barry, one hundred for Harry."

A huge motion picture screen was lowered for a filmed message from President Kennedy. "He has been a supporter of those pieces of legislation which have done the most for our people," said the face on the screen " . . . a leader on behalf of the program for social legislation . . . extreme and patriotic interest in the welfare of our country . . . helped us strengthen our national defense . . . has worked hard for peace . . ."

"He's talking about me," I kept telling myself. It was not easy to believe.

Then Congressman Kirwan introduced President Truman and the fireworks of the evening exploded. The day before, at the airport, Mr. Truman had gone out of his way to praise President Kennedy's civil rights program to reporters and, at the same time, expressed his disapproval of intermarriage between Negroes and whites. At the appreciation dinner Mr. Truman chose to elaborate.

"If the Northern busybodies would stay home and clean up their own backyard, the rest of the country will obey its laws," he said. "The argument on civil rights has been stirred up by Boston and New England demagogues. The War Between the States was brought about by old Harriet Beecher Stowe and William Lloyd Garrison. Those Southerners are anxious to do what the law requires. They want to give equal rights to the Negroes and they are going to do it and nobody is going to stop them doing it. You can be sure of that. They showed that in 1861."

Mr. Truman also had some harsh words to say about permissive parents.

"The youngsters who are running about the country trying to institute mob rule," he declared, "were raised on the nutty theory of let the child grow like a weed with no home discipline. It is a lazy way to raise a family.

"These young rioters were not spanked enough as they grew up. The police should be furnished with nice, old-fashioned butter paddles and should be authorized to use them in the place intended for spankings."

Whether spankings are the most intelligent cure for juvenile delinquency and whether the South, left to itself, will insure equal rights for Negroes are matters on which I entertain some serious reservations. But my admiration for Mr. Truman's courage in getting up and saying whatever is on his mind, no matter what the public relations considerations may be, admits of no reservations whatsoever.

By the time Mr. Truman had finished talking I was sure of one thing. The speech I had prepared for that evening was never going to be made. Instead I told the 1,200 guests,

"I wish very, very much that my dad, Judge Stephen M. Young of Norwalk, and my mother were alive and here tonight. My dad, who was a great story teller, would have been amused by everything that was said about me and my mother would have believed every word. Before she died a few years ago in Norwalk at the age of ninety-four, she gave me some very good advice. I can remember she said to me, 'Pet, don't talk when your mouth is full of mush and milk.' I am telling you, Mr. Truman, my dear friends, my mouth is full, my heart is in my mouth and I am going to follow the advice of my mother and say to each one of you here, you Senators who have come from far places to manifest your affection for my wife and me, and who have said all those fine things about me, and to President Truman who took a long ride from his state to be here and who is returning home tomorrow morning—to him and to all of you with my heart in my mouth, all I can say is thank you, thank you very, very much and may God be with you until we meet again."

And I wondered how it could be that all these people had assembled in Cleveland to pay tribute to me and to urge me to run for the Senate again, when six years earlier the politicians had thought I had as much chance of getting into the Senate as Grandma Moses had of becoming Miss America.

CHAPTER 2

⌇ *In the summer of 1957 there were no crowds at the door of my home in Cleveland pleading with me to go to Washington as junior Senator from Ohio. There were no huge pictures of me hanging on display in the hotel ballrooms of the city. There were no tributes. Although I had served four terms as Congressman-at-large from my state and been active in politics over four decades, had served in the House of Representatives under two Presidents, had helped to frame and transform into law a good share of pivotal legislation in times of trouble and stress, I could hardly claim that my name was a household word in the state.*

To be perfectly honest, the initiative to run came from me. And what motivated me was the thought of John W. Bricker going back to the Senate to represent the people of my state.

Bricker's voting record was deplorable. Even his integrity was questionable in my judgment. The very day he became a United States Senator, in January 1947, he organized his own law firm. In the years when Bricker was a Senator, his law firm was retained by the Pennsylvania Railroad for large sums of money. It is interesting that during that same period the Administration bill to establish the St. Lawrence Seaway was supported by every single Ohio Congressman, Republican and Democrat alike—except Senator Bricker. Bricker—entirely by coincidence, I am sure—always kept the needs of the railroads uppermost in his mind.

Now, Senator Taft was a conservative and Barry Goldwater is a conservative, to say the least, but neither of them ever pretended to bleed for the needy or the downtrodden or the dispossessed or the helpless. Both were honest men—men of principle even though the principle might be classified by some of us as misguided. But I was never convinced that Senator Bricker had any principles that couldn't be sacrificed to some special interest or consideration. And so I thought it might be something of a public service to the citizens of Ohio to show how they were being misrepresented.

If you want to be a United States Senator, the first thing you do—in Ohio, at least—is declare your party and collect signatures from a thousand bona fide members of it representing at least a third of the eighty-eight counties in the state. You have to be sure they are registered voters. Then you get the state party secretary to certify that you have accredited signatures. You pay a fee of fifty dollars which goes into the state treasury.

I assume by now you have persuaded the top leaders of your party that you are the right man for the job. If you can get one or more of them to declare the country cannot go on without you, it may prove helpful.

In the state of Ohio, supposing you get nominated and are not swamped by the opposition, you can contribute to your own campaign a total of $4,000. (My colleague, Senator Clair Engle of California, informed me his campaign to win election as United States Senator in California cost his campaign committee three-quarters of a million dollars. Of course, everything costs more in California.) I hasten to add that the $4,000 Ohio law permits each Senatorial candidate to spend from his personal funds will not come close to being enough money to get you elected; it probably won't even pay your telephone bill. But there are ways around this. Your wife can contribute, and your sister and your brother. Your party can spend money. So can your campaign committee.

26

Then you campaign. You drive and you take trains and you go to big towns and little hamlets and big meetings and small meetings until you are hard put to know where you are and what is the purpose of the meetings. The one thing you are grateful for is that you only have to cover the 4,972 square miles of Ohio instead of the 262,840 of the state of Texas. You eat chicken and peas and mashed potatoes and more fruit cup than you would believe it possible to swallow. You smile when you are tired, shake hands with people you can't quite place, hold debates with men you wouldn't let through the door of your home if you had your personal say. You go to steer roasts and sit on platforms awaiting your turn, sure you've forgotten every word of your speech. You see reporters at their convenience and answer endless questions with no chance to look up or think out the correct answers, remembering that should the questions stop coming and the crowds stop listening and the peace and quiet you so long for actually arrive, you would be a miserable, lonely, deserted and defeated man.

Commencing in the early summer of 1958 I waged an intensive and active personal campaign throughout the length and breadth of Ohio. We spent very little money, but the energy I expended was almost unbelievable. However, there were no invitations for TV appearances. It was not until the election was approaching that reporters were assigned to interview me or take down my speeches. No one except myself seemed to imagine that I had a chance to win. And there was a time when I was terribly depressed and sad; my son Stephen Junior died of cancer in September.

A Cleveland lawyer and Democratic politician, Joseph Silber, had looked me up and suggested I withdraw in favor of Dr. William Stevenson, the president of Oberlin College. He said, "Steve, you haven't a chance. Why not withdraw and let us nominate Dr. Stevenson who is a relative of Adlai?" I said, "Joe, you know I have always believed in

27

open primaries. I never believed in having candidates' nominations fixed in a smoke-filled room. If Dr. Stevenson chooses to run for this nomination, I say 'come on in, the water's fine.'" Joe said, "He'll beat you." I said, "If he should defeat me in the primaries I would support him for election. But he won't."

One of the popular misconceptions about Congressmen is that they herd together like actors or newspapermen, visiting each other's homes, stepping out in groups for dinner, for nightclubbing—that because they are colleagues on the floor of Congress they must be intimates. This may be true of some Representatives and Senators. It has never been true of me.

Now, Frank J. Lausche, who was at that time one of our Ohio Senators, and I had crossed paths in Cleveland. I had consulted him on political matters and was on friendly terms with him. Later he was appointed municipal judge and still later was elected to the Common Pleas Court, where I occasionally appeared before him in lawsuits. In 1941 he ran for mayor of Cleveland and I actively campaigned for him. In 1944 he was elected Governor of Ohio. He was defeated in 1946 when he ran again, but in 1948 he returned to the Governor's Mansion. During the forties I was a Congressman-at-large and whenever Governor Lausche called on me for assistance in state matters I went out of my way to do whatever I could.

Lausche by temperament was politically independent like myself. He had been a hard working and very effective mayor of Cleveland. Yet we were not drawn to each other. In 1945, when President Truman appointed Harold Burton to the Supreme Court, a number of Ohio lawyers wrote to Governor Lausche asking him to choose me to fill the vacancy in the Senate. Lausche answered them cordially, but he went ahead and appointed James W. Huffman to fill the empty seat. Huffman was defeated when he ran for election in 1946. In 1958, Lausche vigorously supported Mike DiSalle,

28

who was running for Governor, but he made no mention of my candidacy.

Meanwhile, the time was getting closer for me to file for the nomination, which is done during the first few days in February. In order to get my thousand bona fide signatures, I sent petitions to the eighty-eight Democratic county chairmen in the state. With each nominating petition I enclosed a two dollar bill. This was no violation of the law. You can pay people to secure signatures for you if you wish. Every petition has enough spaces for twenty-five signatures. I was eager to get petitions from forty counties to be sure that I could at least fill the requirements.

When all the petitions came back I had some four thousand signatures. I filled out my forms, gathered up my petitions and took the whole bundle to State Secretary Ted W. Brown, in Columbus. I paid the money in cash and got a receipt for it and a receipt for the petitions. Then I went home and hoped for the best.

Shortly before that another Democratic friend suggested I announce my withdrawal as a candidate for the nomination so that former Senator Tom Burke could announce his candidacy. He said, "Tom has been a fine mayor of Cleveland and would have strong newspaper support."

I snapped back,

"Well, I'm definitely not going to withdraw. It may be that Tom Burke would secure more votes in Cuyahoga County, but there are eighty-seven other counties in Ohio. If he sent you to see me you go back and tell him he could have beaten George Bender for the Senate if he had worked half as hard to win before election day as he worked for a recount afterward. You tell Tom Burke if he wants to beat Steve Young in Ohio he better get off the bar stool at the Cleveland Athletic Club and even if he did that, he wouldn't come close."

Tom Burke was appointed United States Senator by Governor Frank J. Lausche following the death of Senator Robert A. Taft. No sooner had he been appointed than he was compelled to commence his campaign for election in November 1954. He was defeated by the late George H. Bender by a fraction of 1 percent of the vote. Afterwards Senator Bender referred to himself as "Landslide Bender."

Actually, Tom Burke never filed. I hadn't seriously expected he would, and if he had, I'd have beaten him badly. I have never forgotten that shortly after Burke was appointed Senator he had complained that his phone rang too often at night and too many people were asking for autographs. A political writer in Cleveland warned him that a time might come when the telephone wouldn't ring any more and nobody would ask for his autograph; then he would long for the good old days.

No Democrat filed in opposition to me for nomination at the Democratic primary in May 1958. Talk of opposition subsided, perhaps because of my determination not to withdraw but more likely because very few, if any, thought there was much prospect of defeating John W. Bricker. Mr. Bricker had served as attorney general of Ohio and governor for three terms, establishing a record for future Ohio G. O. P. governors to shoot at, and was his party's candidate for Vice-President of the United States. He had never been defeated and apparently nobody believed he ever would be. We were both unopposed in our respective primaries. His total vote in the Republican primary exceeded mine in the Democratic primary by approximately 100,000.

The primary took place on May 6, 1958, and the campaign began. People were already saying, "Steve Young is so insignificant that Lausche, his fellow Democratic Senator, won't even support him!" During the campaign two huge Democratic meetings in Middletown and Warren had as speakers Senator Lausche and Mike DiSalle, our candidate for governor. They made fine speeches of approximately a half hour

30

each. I was not invited to speak for even two mintues. Had I attended, perhaps I would have been invited to take a bow. At other meetings, particularly when we had a number of candidates touring the state, I drove in the caravan.

As a rule Mike DiSalle would be one of the early speakers and then, of course, would leave for another meeting. When he left, the newspaper reporters usually left with him. Then, customarily, the meeting chairman would go down the whole line (including the candidates for lieutenant-governor, secretary of state, state treasurer), finally reaching me.

One morning the first meeting was a well-attended breakfast in New Lexington. As it happened, I arrived first of all the candidates on the state ballot. There were about eight more meetings scheduled that day. Quite a crowd had already gathered. I hoped, since I was running for an office usually regarded as at least equal to that of Governor, I would be among the first speakers. The county chairman called on a couple of candidates. Then he called on Mike DiSalle, who spoke and then departed for his next engagement. When DiSalle left he took with him six or seven newspapermen and much of the audience.

But the chairman even called on some judicial and local candidates, then the candidates for lieutenant-governor and state treasurer. As each candidate finished, he left immediately for the next meeting and with each one a substantial segment of the audience left, too. Finally, I went up to the county chairman and said in as controlled and quiet a voice as I could muster, "I would like to be called on. I would like to speak." He replied, "I'll reach you in due time."

Just then Mark McElroy, who was candidate for Attorney General, came running in late to the meeting. He was ushered to the platform at once. When McElroy wound up his remarks, more of the audience proceeded to the exits. The chairman left with McElroy. Seven very patient ladies who had heard all the speeches were still seated. Before they could get away, I stood up, introduced myself, made my speech, and the meeting was over.

This is a worm's-eye view of some meetings on the state-wide caravan. If I was ever favored by a county chairman, recollection of that meeting escapes me.

Wherever I went I matched my record of eight years in the House against Bricker's eleven years in the Senate. I called him "an old-line, negative-voting Republican," among other things. I said there would be no conflict of interest if I ever got into the Senate—no dancing to the tunes played by railroad lobbies. I made two definite promises to the citizens of Ohio in most of my speeches throughout the summer and fall of 1958: I would publicly disclose all my financial holdings so that citizens could judge for themselves whether I was actuated by personal interest in casting any of my votes, and I would neither directly nor indirectly practice law. I would devote full time to my duties as United States Senator.

Now, Bricker's record of success in politics was nearly unbroken. There was almost never a ballot in a whole generation that had not borne his name. He had been Governor of Ohio three times. In 1946 he won his Senate seat by a majority of 320,000; in 1952, by 340,000. He dismissed my accusations about his favoring the railroads as "that old chestnut."

The backing Bricker got from the press was sometimes rather curious. The Dayton *Daily News* supported him because they said neither of us was much good, but "it is customary at the *News* to suggest the re-election of incumbents when other factors seem equal in a political contest. This at least has the virtue of consistency. On that basis we see Senator Bricker as the better choice in November."

Meanwhile, the incumbent was trotting out all the Republican arguments favoring the accumulation of wealth by the few at the expense of the many. On agriculture, he favored the removal of acreage controls. He wanted to keep

"the Government out of" education. Of course, by current conservative standards Senator Bricker might be considered a dangerous leftist. After all, when I was campaigning against him, he said he was in favor of increasing social security benefits, selling farm surpluses abroad, and he supported "Atoms for Peace." Obviously, a radical! Yet "Honest John" remained the darling of the reactionaries.

One of the big issues of the campaign centered around a "right to work" law that Bricker endorsed, although initially, in conferences with Republican leaders, he had opposed placing it on the ballot. Some people say the only reason I was elected was because I opposed that law, meaning apparently that the "only" reason the people of Ohio voted for me was because of my liberal political sentiments! If that is the case, I rest content. I would hate to be elected to office because of my reactionary sentiments, as Bricker had been all those years.

The law that Mr. Bricker favored and I opposed would have provided for an amendment which read: "No employer or labor organization shall deny or abridge the right to work by requiring membership in or non-membership in, or payment or non-payment of money to a labor organization as a condition of employment or continued employment" in the state of Ohio. Translated into workaday English, Bricker's proposal, known at that time, as Issue No. 2, simply meant that the hard-won right of the American worker to seek better pay and more decent working conditions through union membership would be crippled and the position of labor might slide back to what it had been in the days of the sweatshops of the nineteenth century. Collective bargaining in the state of Ohio would be seriously weakened.

In my campaign speeches I pointed out that while Mr. Bricker had been a Senator for a long time he was not actually in the Senate as often as he might have been. He had missed fifty out of two hundred and two roll calls that very

33

year. Although he boasted of his activities as a member of the Joint Committee on Atomic Energy, he had attended only twelve of thirty-six meetings held by that committee during the previous session of Congress.

No matter what John Bricker said, the general attitude of the Democratic party seemed to be that he was too formidable an opponent to lick—until I heard that Harry Truman would be campaigning for some Senatorial candidates around the country. I telephoned him and learned that he would be able to come to Cleveland around the middle of October.

My staff immediately asked Ray T. Miller, the Democratic county chairman, or boss of Cuyahoga County, to arrange a dinner where former President Truman would be the principal speaker. It seemed like a wonderful occasion for a big fund-raising affair. Mr. Miller, however, informed us soon afterwards that any funds raised in the county would have to go to the county organization. This would have been of little benefit to my campaign, and we decided instead to have President Truman speak at the Armory in Akron. In making the arrangements, my committee and I paid out 500 dollars. Instead of benefiting from a money-raising affair, I was out 500 dollars. It was the best political investment I ever made.

Mr. Truman arrived in Cleveland early Friday, October 14. There was a reception in his suite to which so many admirers came to shake his hand, and incidentally mine, it appeared that my campaign was beginning to get off the ground.

My colleagues and I cheered up as soon as we came into contact with Mr. Truman. He said outright he thought I was going to beat John Bricker; he even predicted my majority—more than 94,000, he said. Late that afternoon I found myself with the former President as part of a motorcade that roared through every traffic light, sirens blaring, to the

Sheraton-Mayflower in Akron. There, at a dinner for some twenty dignitaries including the mayor of Akron, Law Director of Cleveland Ralph S. Locher (now mayor of Cleveland) and Akron political leaders, Mr. Truman continued to generate an atmosphere of affirmation for my campaign.

At 7:30 we left the hotel and drove to the Armory where the former President spoke to a standing-room-only crowd. He told the rally, attended by 3,500 people, "Don't get Deweyitis because that is the worst disease in the world. The bandwagon will go by and you will wake up in the morning and find yourself defeated." President Truman added, "When you hear a politician term himself 'Honest John,' run home and lock the henhouse door."

Performing in his best "give 'em hell" fashion, Truman told the crowd that President Eisenhower was trying to run the country from a golf course. The overflow audience interrupted him time after time with applause and cheers and shouts of encouragement. There were many members of the rubber unions in town and they applauded the loudest when he denounced the Republicans for "trying to smear the entire labor movement because it's had a few crooks and racketeers." He urged defeat of the right-to-work issue which, he said, should have been called the "right-to-wreck-the-unions." When my reluctant supporters in the Democratic party heard Mr. Truman and saw my well-wishers carrying signs that said "Elect Stephen M. Young," they began to have second thoughts.

Before coming to Akron Mr. Truman spoke at a convention of the International Brotherhood of Electrical Workers in Cleveland. He asked me to accompany him to that meeting. Of course I did. He was given a tremendous ovation. He urged those in attendance to vote for me. On the following day, Mr. Truman took a brisk morning walk, after which he spent hours, it seemed to me, making radio and television spot announcements and television film clippings in support

35

of my candidacy. He seemed to do this willingly, in fact gladly. Then we proceeded to Columbus where there was a big Democratic rally featuring former President Truman and Speaker Sam Rayburn. I made a short speech and was most cordially greeted. I acknowledged that this was due largely to Mr. Truman. At the hotel, just before going to the meeting Mr. Truman said, "I'm going to call the Madam." Then he looked at his watch and said, "Oh, no. It's ten minutes to six and she'd give me hell for not waiting for the night rates."

Truman asked me what the Democratic Senatorial campaign committee was doing for me. I told him I was regularly getting telegrams and letters from the committee and its chairman, Senator George Smathers. He looked shocked. "Is that all!" he exclaimed. He immediately said, "I'm going to Washington tomorrow and the first thing I do, I'm going to see George Smathers and tell him and those other so-and-so's to send you some real money. You're going to win." A few days later my first check came from the committee. Incidentally, soon after that I made a hurried trip to Washington, having first made an appointment to see Paul Butler, chairman of the Democratic National Committee. At the appointed time I was in his reception room. After thirty or forty minutes I was ushered into his private office. When I expressed the hope that he would have a couple of thousand dollars contributed to my campaign, he looked at me coldly in the manner I suspect a Mississippi banker would look at a Negro sharecropper seeking a loan. I returned to my campaign still confident and hopeful, but with no further encouragement from Washington.

In October, Senator Wayne Morse of Oregon and I turned up in Warren, Ohio, to attack Bricker on the right-to-work amendment. Senator Morse warned his listeners that right-to-work laws in Ohio would be just the beginning of a campaign to tear down social security and unemployment compensation and turn back the clock on all the gains that had been made by the workers of this country since the depression of the 1930's. I called Bricker's move to curb the unions a gigantic hoax. I questioned whether Mr. Bricker could pose as a friend of labor and at the same time perpetrate on the working people of Ohio a proposal I called then, and still call, "sheer hokum and deliberate fraud."

Meanwhile, the Republicans were spending more and more money. Bricker kept appearing on TV and radio. There were billboards everywhere clamoring for his election. There were none for me. They were mighty fine political billboards and looked awfully persuasive.

On the Saturday preceding Election Day it is traditional for candidates to appear before the City Club of Cleveland and debate the issues. Throughout the campaign Bricker would not meet with me at a metropolitan newspaper office or appear on a radio or television program preceding or following my appearance, his strategy apparently being to ignore my very existence. "Young doesn't amount to anything," he said. "I won't meet with him." Nevertheless, he agreed to the City Club debate.

The debate took place before the crowded City Club and was broadcast by radio. On the preceding Thursday the political writer of the Cleveland *News* had persisted in asking for an advance release of my speech. In 1950 I had given this same newspaper an advance release of the arguments I intended to make against George H. Bender, my Republican opponent for Congressman-at-large. Bender put it over me like a tent in that debate and I always thought he had the advance copy of my remarks. Because of this, I picked out paragraphs left over from earlier campaign speeches and put them together in some manner. I had no intention of using any of them. During the debate I hoped to speak first for twenty minutes and reserve the final ten minutes for rebuttal. I lost the toss of the coin, but Senator Bricker chose to speak second, so I had my way even though I lost the toss. I prepared my remarks as carefully as I would the final arguments in an important law suit. In fact, this was probably the most important "case" I ever argued. It appeared to me as we walked downstairs and into the hall before the debate that my opponent was somewhat nervous. He spoke of debating before in the same club with Charles Sawyer and Jim Huffman and said that now they were his best friends. I said nothing, but I thought, "Buster, after I've spoken ten seconds you won't want me for a best friend."

As I assaulted Senator Bricker's dignity, he grew red in the face. Each of us spoke for half an hour.

Said Bricker: "Unbalanced budgets and national government are mortgaging the future of America and depriving our children of their rightful heritage."

Said I: "Senator Bricker is an obstructionist who blocks, sabotages and whittles down programs to abolish slums and house people decently."

Said he: "One of the primary issues in the next session of Congress will be the budget. Deficit financing can only lead to disaster. It is the most insidious and dangerous form of taxation."

Said I: "Mr. Bricker is the darling of the business lobbyists. He tells you today that he is for social security. This is a lot of nonsense. It was Mr. Bricker who termed social security state socialism. Will he deny that statement now? My opponent symbolizes the far right of Republican reaction, the kind of Republicanism which failed to produce legislative protection for the little man. This kind of Republicanism believes that unorganized workers should sell their labor as individuals and without collective bargaining."

Said he: "I am against aid to Communist countries and I also believe that much of the non-military aid which we have scattered around the world has been wasted."

Said I: "This is the man who voted against the Greek-Turkish aid bill. He voted three times against military aid to Europe in its fight to resist Communist aggression."

Said he: "In industry, over one-half billion dollars was saved last year. This is only a beginning."

Said I: "One of his first acts as Senator was to oppose an increase in minimum wages from 40 cents to 60 cents an hour."

Said he: "The budget could have been balanced last year. More governments have fallen because of inflation than ever collapsed before the onslaught of hostile armies."

Said I: "The G. O. P. Senator does not believe in unemployment compensation, but he does believe in unemployment."

I suspected strongly when the debate was over that I was going to win the election, even though President Eisenhower had recently come to Ohio to speak up for Bricker and the Republican candidates for Congress.

My hopes rose even higher one evening when I was scheduled to speak in Lima, Ohio. When I left the speaker's platform I was introduced to Paul Block, the owner and publisher of the Toledo *Blade,* and to his city editor. I knew the top staff members of the *Blade* were down there to look me over. Shortly afterwards, the *Blade* gave me its editorial endorsement. It was the only metropolitan paper in Ohio which did so.

My headquarters in the Manger Hotel consisted of two little rooms. We had one paid helper and few volunteers. On election night we rented a larger room on the mezzanine floor. When I arrived with my wife, daughter and granddaughter, the place was almost deserted. A little while later I stopped at a public telephone booth and called Harold Stern, who was standing by ready to tabulate returns as they were telephoned in. I said, disguising my voice, "This is Zindrich of the twenty-ninth ward, precinct P. Do you wish any returns?" (The twenty-ninth ward is heavily Democratic.)

"Oh, yes."

"Well, here are the returns as far as Governor and Senator are concerned. DiSalle 285, O'Neill 88; Young 136, Bricker

39

241." I could hear the sharp intake of Harold's breadth. "Is that accurate?" he asked tensely.

"Yes, indeed. That's the correct report." I hung up quickly before he could hear me laughing. Soon afterwards I went over to the Manger and asked Harold if there were any returns. "Only one," he said.

"Is it good?" I had a struggle to keep a straight face.

"Wait until another return comes in," he answered.

When the returns *did* come in I started ahead and stayed ahead. With only fifty precincts from Cuyahoga County reported in, I was ahead by some 30,000 votes. In my pocket was a telegram addressed to Bricker which read, "I'm extending my congratulations and best wishes to you. Ohio citizens have spoken by their votes and I wish you every success, good health and happiness during your forthcoming six years in the Senate."

Around 11:00 p.m. there was a call for me from Edward R. Murrow in New York. He said he believed I was going to win and asked for a statement.

In the state of Ohio the polls close officially at 6:30 p.m. on Election Day. In urban areas, though, there is always a line of late voters, so they stay open an hour or so longer. If you come in to vote at 7:15 there is no one to say you can't vote because you weren't around at 6:30. They don't have voting machines in all parts of Ohio, either. In some states political leaders on both sides try to hold back the machine votes by not reporting them promptly to the secretary of state, knowing that there are many precincts still to report even as late as eleven at night. I told Mr. Murrow, therefore, that I preferred not to make a statement. I remembered a candidate in 1956 with an overwhelming lead in the early precincts who issued statements and got his picture in the papers—and then the returns from the suburbs wiped him out.

By 11:30 our once-deserted little headquarters in the

40

Manger was beginning to fill up with new-found friends. Our small supply of refreshments—we had put what little money we had into Cokes and food—was wiped out. Early returns were in and, with only fifty precincts from Cuyahoga County reported, showed me leading.

DEMOCRATIC SWEEP OUSTS BRICKER, read a streamer headline in the Cleveland *Press* the following noon. TIDAL WAVE OF DEMOCRATIC VOTES HAS PUT MIKE DISALLE IN THE GOVERNOR'S CHAIR AND STEPHEN M. YOUNG IN THE SENATE.

"DiSalle, fifty-year-old former Toledo mayor and ex-director of the Office of Price Stabilization, trimmed C. William O'Neill by 460,000 votes to win the state.

"Young, at sixty-nine a veteran of Ohio political wars, bumped the 'invincible' John William Bricker out of the Senate after twelve years. The 'unbeatable' Bricker was closed out by some 155,000 votes in the state.

"One lone Republican, Secretary of State Ted M. Brown, survived the switch which put the state house, the legislature and many of the county courthouses into Democratic hands."

The headline in the *Plain Dealer* was: YOUNG AND DI-SALLE ELECTED. RIGHT TO WORK ISSUE BEATEN. AMENDMENTS SWAMPED BY 400,000 VOTES.

It had taken a while for the *Plain Dealer* to give in. In their first edition after midnight, they described me as leading but not elected. The city editor had been told I was elected, but he didn't believe it!

Early on Election Day Mr. Truman had called me from Washington. "I hear you waged a hell of a campaign," he said, and predicted I was going to win by 94,000 votes. I think that was one of the few conservative statements Truman ever made. When all the returns were in, my plurality was more than 155,000.

41

CHAPTER 3

⚑ *On an afternoon in late December of 1958 I walked down a gray corridor on the first floor of the Old Senate Office Building, which sometimes seems to me to have been scaled to the size of giants rather than people, searching for the office of Senator Bricker.*

That office from now on was going to be mine.

When I walked into the reception room I was greeted by a horrifying sight of files and furniture jammed every which way. There were three or four rooms, but it took a bit of investigating before I could even locate the walls. The place looked completely uninhabitable, and I was wondering rather gloomily how I was ever to get it in shape so I could work there when a newspaper photographer came along and asked me if I would mind putting my name up on the door—he wanted a picture. Since this had to be done anyway, I was happy to oblige. It wasn't easy to get hold of a screwdriver, but somehow the plate went up. Our government can rise to any emergency.

With my name actually visible on the entrance door, I began to believe that I really had beaten Bricker, as everybody had said I wouldn't. Now I would have to justify the victory. Over the years when I was a Congressman-at-large I had been content with my allotment of one secretary and a few stenographic helpers—no administrative assistant, no research assistant, no complicated system of buzzers or telephones that light up, or any of the other appurtenances which make the daily life of a Senator at once wonderfully convenient and hopelessly complicated. Now I was given a liberal allowance which enabled me to assemble a staff of fourteen. The first thing to do, I decided, was to clear a space where somebody could sit down and hold an interview. I won't say that my predecessor deliberately sabotaged his headquarters to make my first days as his successor as unpleasant as they could be, but it certainly looked that way.

The size of the staff a Senator is entitled to is determined by the population of his state. The staff of an Ohio Senator, as I am perhaps too fond of saying, is smaller than that of his colleague from California but larger than that of his Alaskan colleague. When we began to work the following Monday I had two personal secretaries, "Gabby" Gandal of Cleveland Heights who had been employed in December, and Eva Robinson. Eva had been a public stenographer in the office building I occupied in Cleveland. Then there was Herb Jolovitz, a lawyer from Canton, who had worked hard for me during the campaign. A week before my election I had been impressed with his good sense and administrative ability. I had called him at his home in Canton shortly after the returns came in. He has proven himself indispensable to me ever since. Another extremely useful person on my staff from the beginning was Albert J. (Bud) Chaney, who had worked for twenty-four years on Capitol Hill. He had come to Washington to work for Senator Vic Donahey, a Democrat, and had continued as a Senatorial staff assistant under Senator John W. Bricker. He was the only one on my payroll with previous experience on the Hill, and he set to work at once getting the rooms put into shape, the floors recarpeted and office supplies sent up from the stationery room. After opening a stack of mail that turned out to be mostly congratulatory, we set to work hiring the rest of the staff.

44

One of the first official gatherings I attended was a Democratic caucus. These meetings do not take place in a pool of tears like the caucus in *Alice in Wonderland,* but they sometimes wind up that way. At this preliminary meeting the Democratic Senators were welcomed by Majority Leader Lyndon Johnson. None of us dreamed then what a mighty responsibility destiny had in store for him, but even at that time, if you had asked me, I would have said he was fully equal to it. Senator Clair Engle of California and I received warm praise from the Majority Leader—after all, we had returned Governor "Goody" Knight of California and Senator John Bricker of Ohio to private life.

There were many other caucuses. There was a myriad of details to be settled before our office could operate efficiently. There were interviews with reporters—Bob Crater and Lowell Bridwell of Scripps-Howard, Bob Hoyt of the Akron *Beacon-Journal,* George Jenks of the Toledo *Blade* and Bud Silverman, Ed Kernan, Phil Goulding and John Leacacos of the Washington staff of the Cleveland *Plain Dealer.* (I had served in Italy with Major John Leacacos.) They would ask me how I found Washington after an absence of a number of years, what committee assignments I had asked for, how my wife liked the capital. I wonder if I can still answer those questions!

I found Washington under the heavy hand of President Eisenhower and not yet quite recovered from the stupefaction that had set in under the terrorist influence of Senator Joe McCarthy. It struck me as a timid and troubled city, although it was not to stay that way for very long.

Before I ever took my seat in the Senate chamber I put my foot down on two things. I refused to serve on the District of Columbia committee. I said, perhaps rather presumptuously, that having been elected United States Senator by citizens of Ohio, I did not propose to serve as city councilman for Washington. I also said in the strongest language that I would do everything in my power to prevent the confirmation of a judgeship for C. William O'Neill, who had been defeated in the Ohio gubernatorial contest by Mike DiSalle. C. William O'Neill is now a judge of the Ohio Supreme Court, a respected and competent public servant; probably I should not have voiced any objection to him. There was really little likelihood that President Eisenhower would nominate him for a judgeship; in my opinion, former Senator Bricker would not have recommended him.

The particular committees I asked to serve on were the Aeronautical and Space Sciences, Agriculture and Forestry, and Public Works. I was appointed to all three.

I was rather unhappy later on as a member of the Committee on Agriculture and Forestry. I had hoped very much to be helpful since Ohio is a great agricultural state. I attended meetings faithfully, but it turned out to be time wasted, for most of the hours were taken up by our chairman, Allen Ellender of Louisiana, in a series of monologues. The Ohio Farm Bureau, which is the powerful group in my state, is really the Chamber of Commerce for the wealthier farmers. And it was disturbing to find that, as a rule, the Bureau did not properly represent the interests of the small family farmers. Its lobbyists almost invariably favored Republican-sponsored proposals. Later they opposed every farm program offered during President Kennedy's administration.

As for the reporter's question, "Does your wife like Washington?" she seemed to love it. I had married Rachel Bell of North Carolina in March 1957, five years after the death of Ruby Louise Dawley of Cleveland, who had been my constant companion since she became my bride in 1911. Ruby bore me two sons—Stephen M. Young, III, who died in 1958, and Richard Dawley Young—and one daughter, Marjorie Louise (Mrs. Robert Richardson).

Rachel and I were introduced in Fort Lauderdale in the fall of 1956. I don't know which has sustained me more in

46

the years since—her strength or her sense of humor. She was with me on every single trip I took during the Senatorial campaign, when we sometimes covered fifteen different meetings in the course of two days. As for her sense of humor, there is nothing she likes better than to prick the bubble of stupid pretense. Shortly after we were married I remember attending a party in Shaker Heights. A rather affected socialite came over to her and asked in dripping tones if she knew a Mrs. So-and-So in Asheville, North Carolina. "It is so beautiful," she simpered at Rachel, "and you are so fortunate to have been born there." "Listen," my wife replied promptly, "I don't know much about Asheville. I was born and reared in a little town in North Carolina called Mount Olive. The principal social event of that town was when the shoo-fly train came down Main Street at five o'clock each afternoon."

People ask about social life in Washington. "Terrific" would be the answer if a Senator were to attend all functions to which he is invited. Frankly, unless a Senator throws in the sponge and accepts only one-fourth of the invitations, he will be out socially five or six evenings weekly. This might create hardship; for example, inability to see "Gunsmoke," "Wells Fargo," "Maverick" and "Wagon Train," to say nothing of wasting time that's needed to study pending legislation or read Committee reports.

More than a hundred nations have embassies in Washington. Each holds two large receptions a year, plus dinners and cocktail parties to which most Senators are invited. There are at least seventeen state dinners. Among others there are dinners given by the 270 national associations, such as the American Legion, the Veterans of Foreign Wars, the United States Chamber of Commerce and the National Association of Manufacturers. These are registered pressure groups, so called. They filed reports admitting to expenditures of 4 million dollars during 1963. Many of these national associations invite all members of Congress to one dinner a year. In addition, various state associations, labor unions such the Post Office Clerks', and citizens' organizations give dinners, cocktail parties and receptions. They wine and dine Congressmen, and individual members and speakers may discuss legislative proposals they are promoting. At least thirty Senators give dinners or luncheons for their colleagues, and usually Senators give dinners for their own state Congressional delegations, or a Representative throws an affair to which he invites the Senators from his state. In addition, a new horror has been devised—breakfasts, to which Senators are invited. The time stated is generally 8:30 a.m. but, if a Senator attends, he is fortunate to leave by ten o'clock. Furthermore, quite frequently groups from the Senator's own state, visiting in Washington, desire him to lunch or dine with them. These are invitations a Senator appreciates receiving and likes to accept; and in turn he does not keep his own pocketbook padlocked; he wines and dines constituents and throws parties to repay obligations, an American custom we like. Regarding "pressure groups" and various professional and business associations, many Congressmen say "too busy" and are happy to pay for their own meals, and to eat at home one or two evenings a week. Incidentally, irregular working hours with sessions frequently lasting into the night are not conducive to party-giving or party-going. I used to think Perle Mesta was some kind of ballplayer. I would rather watch a re-rerun of an old TV Western in my bathrobe and slippers than bow in at a gaudy reception any time.

I try to make myself available to all callers, particularly those from Ohio, and news reporters are never required to make appointments; I figure they have a job to do, and I try to see them immediately. In the beginning there were the job seekers, especially those put out of work by the results of Election Day. We had a continuous stream of them for a week or so. It didn't take long, either, for the lobbyists to start ganging up. Sometimes it takes the utmost control to react without rage to some of the pressure these people try to put on you.

The Capitol, and in particular the Senate Reception Room, is frequently so crowded with lobbyists that sometimes Capitol policemen should be called on to enable Senators to walk from the elevator to the Senate Chamber. I like to talk to Ohioans, but too frequently lobbying groups from other states seek to present their views, and all this is time-consuming. Lobbying organizations are required to file reports of their expenditures. Senators usually consider that the actual amount spent is at least double the amount reported. According to the authoritative *Congressional Quarterly*, the report shows the following as the "spendingest" lobbies seeking to persuade members of the Congress to go along with their views:

American Medical Association
AFL-CIO (national headquarters)
American Farm Bureau Federation
American Legion
U. S. Savings and Loan Leagues

Many corporation officials have tried to influence my vote on taxes and bills that affected them one way or another. Quite often companies confer the title of vice-president on their Washington representatives to facilitate their access to Congressmen. There is nothing improper about this. Lobbyists are here to stay. If they are well informed, they may be able to convince a Senator or Representative of the merits of their cause. Sometimes to those who try to sway my judgment on legislation which I have thoroughly researched and on which I have very decided convictions, I say, "Look, I'll talk with you, but you're wasting your time and mine. I

49

have studied this matter thoroughly, have spoken out on it and you won't change my mind." There have been days when I have said this to ten people.

A Senator is subject to many flattering temptations. He doesn't have an expense account and if he is offered transportation or gifts or even meals it may seem hard to say no. The price of saying yes, however, is often too steep. Because I am on the Armed Services Committee I can travel back to Ohio on an Air Force plane practically any time I wish. I prefer to go on a commercial line. I don't like to accept favors even from the Air Force.

There are also visits from union leaders. I treat them the same way—impartially. As a Senator I always try to conduct myself as if the possibility of re-election didn't exist. In that way you say what you think is right, not what you assume will get you votes.

The lobbyists of today represent thousands of pressure groups. They use a variety of methods to put pressure on Congressmen. One of their devices is pressure mail, which is easy to spot. Once when I got a thousand letters from various parts of Ohio and every one was addressed "Stephen A. Young," I knew a careless lobbyist had forgotten the middle initial of my name, which comes considerably later in the alphabet. This particular batch of letters was in connection with Senate Bills 1089 and 1197, which had to do with railroads, Without going into the details I will simply say that I was opposing these bills because I believed they would put the *coup de grace* to our railroads as a basic transportation industry.

When a letter refers by number to a forthcoming bill in the Senate, I have reason to suspect it was written at the prompting of a vested interest or a Washington lobbyist.

The letters that influence me are not obvious attempts to put pressure on me in the decisions I make when I vote on a bill, but the personal letters that express the real views and beliefs of the writers as individuals.

When citizens call on me to present their demands, I am always glad to give them as much time as I can. Often I come away having been persuaded by their arguments. In any case, I believe it is my duty to listen; they have usually come a long way to see me. In 1946 a Federal Lobbying Act was passed making it necessary for lobbyists to register and file reports of what they do and what they spend. In 1954 the Supreme Court defined a lobbyist as someone who "has direct communication with a legislator." The trouble is that there doesn't seem to be any limit to the amount of money available for publicity, public relations and propaganda.

In the summer of 1959 the Congress was looking into the possibilities of various bills to curb certain labor abuses. When a bill called the Landrum-Griffin Bill was introduced in the House, one Southern Congressman from an industrial town found that his phone was ringing incessantly; word was out that he was not going to vote for the bill. Actually, he was planning to support a more moderate bill on the same subject which House Speaker Sam Rayburn had approved, and which had a better chance and made more sense. He spent fourteen hours a day trying to explain to the people who called—at home as well as at the office. But they weren't satisfied. Manufacturers, industrialists, Chamber of Commerce officials kept after him. It began to affect him in psychosomatic pains in the arms, shoulders and chest. He said it was worse than when he had served as a combat fighter pilot in the Second World War. He stuck to his guns and was the only man from his state to vote against the bill in question, but he isn't a member of the House of Representatives any more.

Yet in the last few years even the business lobbyists have been made to look like amateurs compared with the powerful Washington lobbyists of the American Medical Association during the fight over medical care for the aged. I wasn't surprised when it started. I was a member of the House back in 1949 when the AMA spent nearly five million dollars to campaign against President Truman's national health insurance program.

Let me hasten to add that the lobbyists don't always get their way. The American Meat Institute tried to stifle the Humane Slaughter Bill in 1958, but they took a licking from the Humane Society of the United States, which didn't employ a single paid lobbyist. And this despite a three-year campaign during which more than a thousand articles, headlines and news stories were printed in the nation's press, and more than four million pieces of literature were distributed.

They tell me that lobbying began before this country even had a government, when various merchants would invite New England representatives to dinner as they were on their way to the first Continental Congress and suggest to them that they steer clear of dangerous ideas on American independence.

The only way I know to retaliate against a pressure group when I consider that legitimate legislation is threatened is to stand up on the floor of the Senate, question the group's intentions and aims, and thus counter with pressures of my own. I think we ought not to stifle our lobbyists, but I do think that every American ought to be alert and sophisticated enough to recognize their motives and tactics. They are one of the prices we pay for being a democracy.

Then there are visitors of another kind, the kind who have to be led away quietly and should be under treatment. There was one man who sent a postcard from Wisconsin, which stated, "I am coming down to punch you in the nose," and he actually came. One day there he was, a man in his eighties, obviously demented, who saw Communists under every bed. One of my assistants tried to talk with him reasonably, but that was impossible. He started calling everybody in sight Communists. He was told I wasn't in and that it would be best for him to leave. Then he got hold of one of my secretaries, "Gabby." She tried to calm him down. When I came up from the Senate floor I was warned about this visitor and told he might get violent. I let him see me anyway. He was very meek and mild, however, standing in the door to my private office. I made it a point to stand close to him, my chest practically against his. He was one of those blabbermouths who will insult a Senator's secretary over the telephone or in person but wilts when confronted by another man. I told him to get out. Evidently, he knew I meant it. He eased out within a second or so. I thought afterwards, if he had really made the trip from Wisconsin to abuse me, he had wasted his money.

During my early days as Senator, I received an Ohio inventor of a space ship. He proceeded to set up an exhibit of numbered cardboard parts. When asked how this device was powered, he said, "I don't have that worked out yet." Then there was the lady who wanted to start a library in the United Nations. She still turns up once in a while. And there was the man who introduced himself as the son of Nobel of Nobel Peace Prize fame. He had a long beard and his precise intention never did become clear to me. And there was another chap who said the FBI was after him. Every time he arrived he would introduce himself as a professor from a different college. He said the FBI had a transistor receiver hidden in his teeth and was out to get him. I had no clear idea what I was expected to do for him, but I do hope he is getting the care he needs.

I guess the biggest mix-up we ever had in my office over a visitor was the time when I was gargling for a sore throat in my office washroom; suddenly I felt myself choking. I couldn't get my breath back. One of the girls on the staff called for a doctor. That afternoon one of our typewriters had gone out of whack and there had been a call for a repair man. During my choking fit a well-dressed man came in carrying a black bag. One of the girls grasped him by the arm and rushed him into my office crying, "Here's the doctor." Unfortunately, in this gentleman's bag there was only equipment for cleaning rollers and adjusting typewriter keys. He had nothing at all for choking fits. But, fortunately for me, by that time I was breathing normally again.

Most of our days are not colorful. I am generally up about six in the morning. My alarm clock is the *Congressional Record*. It is delivered about that time and the sound of its being thrown against my front door or on the front porch invariably awakens me. I fix myself coffee and then put out food for the two cats and Dolly, a Yorkshire terrier. One member of our family is a coal black kitten with a couple of white hairs on her chest named Lili, who has had her home with us since she was a small handful. More recently I picked up a stray kitten at around midnight from the shrubbery in front of an expensive apartment building on Massachusetts Avenue. This little yellow kitten, according to the doorman, had evidently been thrown out of an automobile. Then, some people coming out of the apartment where suites rent from 250 dollars up kicked at her, and she ran again into the shrubbery. The doorman said he was the only one who fed her. She was very thin and frightened but took to me, and she is now a beautiful young cat named Pinkey. Sometimes I wish my life was as placid as the cats'.

Then the Washington *Post* is delivered. I look this over rather quickly. At about seven my wife, whom I regard as a late riser, comes downstairs. By 7:45, as a rule, I'm on my way to the Senate Office Building. If I start after eight o'clock, this drive takes forty-five minutes instead of twenty. En route I listen to music and news on the car radio.

At the office, which is open at eight or before, I immediately look at the mail, then perhaps look over the *Congressional Record* if I have neglected to do this at home.

54

The hours of my staff are staggered. The first group usually gets in about eight. At nine I start answering the mail. My letters have brought me some notoriety, and I like to be at my best when I write them.

In those first days I think I spent a lot of my time trying to master the buzzer system that governs the activities of the Senate. Whenever there is a roll call vote, or quorum call, or the Senate goes into session or adjourns, a buzzer sounds in every office in the New and Old Senate Office Buildings. There is a Senate rule that business can't be conducted unless a quorum—a majority—is present. Actually, for practical purposes, there are seldom more than seven or eight Senators on the floor at one time. It takes a bit of getting used to, to go through the preparations of researching and writing a speech and then to find yourself facing a virtually empty room when the time comes to deliver it. At any time, however, a Senator may suggest the "absence of a quorum." Then the roll must be called. If fewer than fifty Senators answer to their names, the presiding officer announces that a quorum is not present and again the roll is called. If, by the end of this call, a quorum is still not present, then it is up to the sergeant-at-arms to secure the presence of sufficient Senators to make a quorum. Or perhaps the Majority Leader will move, as he has on a few occasions, that the Senate recess or adjourn. There is likely to be a roll call on this question also. A roll call vote is announced by one buzz, a quorum call, which will not be recorded in the *Congressional Record,* by two. This is known as a "dead quorum." Three buzzes are what is called a "live quorum." This means that the presence or absence of a Senator will be recorded in the *Congressional Record.* Three buzzes or bells invariably result in considerably more than fifty-one Senators responding. Four short buzzes indicate adjournment.

In the normal course of a day there may be only ten or fifteen Senators in the chamber, sometimes even fewer. One reason is that committee meetings may be in progress at the same time, and Senators remain in attendance there unless there is a live quorum call. On other occasions the leadership may want to stay on and keep things going, but there is no one on hand to speak. To stall for time, therefore, they suggest absence of a quorum and the clerk will start to call off the names with funereal slowness—perhaps three names a minute. It is really nothing but a stall for time when a speaker is needed, or, in the midst of legislation, when a conference among party leaders becomes necessary. The Majority and Minority Leaders, if not present in the Senate, usually designate an acting leader. His job is to sit at the leadership desk and, in the absence of his leader, watch proceedings, make necessary objections to unanimous consent requests and, if attendance dwindles, suggest the absence of a quorum.

The party leaders may, on occasion, leave the Senate Chamber without designating an acting leader. No advantage is taken by any Senator present. However, there was one incident which occurred in such a situation. A certain Senator, during a period when very few Senators were on the floor and the party leader was absent, demanded recognition from the presiding officer, received it and said, "Mr. President, I ask unanimous consent to abolish the Republican Party." The presiding officer, out of habit, said, "Without objection it is so ordered." Then, grasping the content of the request, he backtracked fast. Senator Kuchel recently said, "That request was almost agreed to. That's what caused me pain." This performance boomeranged later. A Republican Senator, finding no Democratic Senator present, asked unanimous consent that Louisiana be put out of the Union. That was nearly bye-bye Bayou. Such are the hazards of democracy.

The four buzzes for adjournment I envision as causing a good deal of scurrying back to desks in Senate offices, including mine.

56

There is another system of buzzers I don't think I shall ever master. It is on my desk and is meant to summon the various people on my staff. I think I am just beginning to get the hang of it now, when my term is almost over. By pressing all the buttons at once I could summon all fourteen of them, which would eliminate guesswork. Sometimes it's a temptation.

CHAPTER 4

✍ *One thing I noticed early about the United States Senate —it is a much friendlier body than the House of Representatives. I don't agree with some who consider the Senate an exclusive club, but I do think that the cordiality of every Senator toward newcomers is quite marked. It is strange. A Senator has to work much harder than a Representative, and yet the Senate atmosphere is warmer. Perhaps the six-year term has something to do with it.*

I must say, though, that the friendly atmosphere of the Senate did not extend to the White House when General Eisenhower was living there. I had met him in Naples during the war in 1943. I was only a major at that time and one of his many admirers. Of course, there was no reason for him to remember me. As a Senator in 1959 and 1960 I never met him personally, never talked with him, never met his wife. I never set foot in the White House. In fact, I was never invited there.

Within the Senate itself, however, I made many friends. I met a lot of them in the Senate gym. I hadn't been a Senator more than two or three days when I discovered the gym. To it I feel I owe a good part of my health and well-being today. I had an injured shoulder when I first went down there for a workout and a steam bath. When a group of men sit in a hot room for maybe twenty minutes, in so relaxed an atmosphere, they get to know each other very well. Important Senatorial business is frequently discussed. When alone there I read or simply relax.

It is said that my colleague, Senator Lausche, recommended that the Senate swimming pool should be boarded up. I do not agree. It is the practice of most corporations to have exercise rooms or gyms for their officials and employees. Senator Lausche and some other Senators prefer their exercise and recreation on the golf course. I really prefer mine on the tennis courts. Senator Ellender of Louisiana, chairman of the Senate Committee on Agriculture and Forestry, tries to exercise in the gym every day. The story is told that one day the bells rang for a quorum when he had completed exercising and was drying himself following a swim. He dashed out to respond to the quorum call—forgetting he had nothing on but a towel. A gym attendant grabbed him on his way to the elevator.

It may surprise some people to learn that one of the men I count as a close friend in the Senate is Barry Goldwater. I have served on the Armed Services Committee with him, and though I have heard that he is a problem on the Labor and Public Welfare Committee because of his views, which I consider to be pre-McKinley, on the Armed Services Committee he has always worked harmoniously with the rest of us and his views on national defense are respected. That is as it should be. I would be extremely surprised to wake up one morning and learn he had assumed the Presidency of this country while I was asleep, but I like to think that if such a thing happened, many of his more extreme eighteenth and nineteenth century ideas would vanish soon enough. At this time he may advocate sending out our marines from Guantanamo Naval Base and our air power to scatter Castro's militia, but if he were President, his ideas might change; he would without doubt bear in mind that some Americans would be killed and that thousands of Cuban civilians, including women and children, would also be killed. He has many quaint attitudes toward social security and medical care and other legislation, which today he talks against as socialistic. As President, he would have to modify those ideas or forget them. The people of this country would never stand for forfeiting all the gains they have made since the days of FDR. On the other hand, if I were in a military unit, I would have confidence in Barry Goldwater as my officer. He has courage, he is a likeable fellow—a man's man. He is considerate and jovial, and I always marvel at the quick trips he takes all over the country. He is a bug, as I am, on the subject of exercise. There is a photograph of him on my office wall, inscribed "To my friend and dedicated great American, Senator Stephen Young." I am grateful to him for sending that to me.

From the "class of 1959" I have made enduring friendships among the Democratic Senators elected at the same time— Robert C. Byrd of West Virginia, Howard W. Cannon of Nevada, Thomas J. Dodd of Connecticut, Clair Engle of California, Philip A. Hart of Michigan, Vance Hartke of Indiana, Eugene J. McCarthy of Minnesota, Gale W. McGee of Wyoming, Frank E. Moss of Utah, Edmund S. Muskie of Maine, Harrison A. Williams, Jr., of New Jersey, E. L. (Bob) Bartlett and Ernest Gruening of Alaska. When any of us offers an amendment to pending legislation the rest of us— unless the forthcoming bill goes against anyone's conscience —try to help out with our votes. One of the happiest friendships I have had has been with Clair Engle of California. Howard Cannon, Frank Moss, Gale McGee, Ernest Gruening are men I am always glad to see. Gruening and I frequently talk about the "young" ticket of experience since he is somewhat older than I am. We often discuss running for President and Vice-President, respectively, but we can never agree who should be President. I like Bobby Byrd and Alan Bible, Wayne Morse, Clinton Anderson, Ed Muskie, Joe Clark, Bill Proxmire, Everett Jordan, Herman Talmage,

Ralph Yarborough—but why go on. They are good companions. Not all Senators are on close terms with each other, but we come to meet with and know members of our own party better than those of the other.

I had not been in the Senate more than five days when one of my Democratic colleagues came up to me in the hall. "Excuse me, Steve," he said, "but I'd like to approach you on a very important matter. I wouldn't dream of interrupting you, but I think you'll be interested in this. You may have heard that the Senate of the United States is the most exclusive club in the world. I want to tell you about a really exclusive club. We call it the Hideaway and our membership committee has unanimously elected you." I was glad to join for when the Senate session is unduly prolonged, there is usually a relaxed club meeting. Senator Maurine Neuberger is welcome. Senators Everett Jordan, Sam Ervin, Dick Russell and Herman Talmage are about the best storytellers. The only individual not a Senator in attendance, to my recollection, was Tony Celebrezze. I took him to the Hideaway Club off the Senate Chamber on the day before he was confirmed as Secretary of Health, Education and Welfare.

Then we Democrats who were elected in 1958 occasionally have parties at each other's homes. I remember one at the home of Vance Hartke. He had arranged a dinner of Maine lobster. In the process of cooking it one of the stoves exploded. That was also the night we decided to call President Truman around one o'clock in the morning. The former President chatted with us for a while and then he said he thought he would like to go back to sleep. Vance said, "If you're hanging up to save money, that isn't necessary. Steve Young is paying for this call."

One Senator whose life sometimes gets entangled with mine is Senator Milton Young of North Dakota. One evening in the summer of 1959 I was called out of the Senate Chamber. "There is an important call for you from the White House," the page said. I hurried to the phone. The call was coming from President Eisenhower's office. The woman who was talking described herself as an administrative assistant. "I'm so glad I was able to get you," she said. She then started going on and on about a complicated set of difficulties which I was unable to disentangle in any way. Finally, it occurred to me that she had the wrong Senator Young. I never did find out what the trouble was.

His mail and mine are mixed up often. Once in a while one of his visitors comes to see me or vice versa. Strangely enough, he had trouble with his right arm at about the same time I had trouble with mine. I injured my arm during a warm-up for a tennis match in Shaker Heights in May 1958, when I tried a fancy backhand. The crack was so distinct my opponent heard it on the other side of the net. Almost immediately I was driven to the hospital. I was waiting to see the doctor when a Negro woman brought in her eleven-year-old son whose leg was bleeding. The doctor told the tearful woman, "You'll have to wait until I attend to this man." I said, "Listen, doctor, that boy is bleeding. I can wait." Later I went to another hospital and then to a bone specialist in Cleveland.

I'd nearly recovered from this injury to my right shoulder when in October around ten at night at Franklin, hurrying into a schoolhouse to address a political meeting, I tripped over a rolled rubber mat which held open a door into a darkened hall. In addition to a gash at my temple and a black eye, ligaments in my right shoulder were badly torn. In the course of speech-making from then on, including my debate with Senator Bricker at the City Club of Cleveland, I was unable to raise my right arm above the shoulder. This disability persisted for months despite treatment. Milton Young's accident happened in an automobile. Mine put a crimp in my tennis game and his kept him off the golf course.

Both of us also were the victims of the usual rumors when anything happens to a Senator more than fifty years old. If you come down with a cold, if your hair starts thinning out, if you cut your finger, the rumors fly. "He's weak—he's no good any more—he's through." They write you off. Members of Congress realize that there are always eager beavers waiting at the sidelines to succeed them.

The rumors may be dangerous or they may be funny. I am reminded of an incident many years ago when a Senator who shall be nameless got a telephone call around midnight from the manager of the Willard Hotel where he was occupying a room. "Senator," said the manager, "you have a woman in that room with you and you are registered as a single occupant. I thought I should inform you, sir, that the house detective is quite disturbed." To this the Senator said, "I'd have you know that the young lady is my secretary and I don't appreciate being disturbed." With that he banged down the receiver. A few minutes later the manager rang the room again. "Senator," he murmured, "I apologize once more for disturbing you, but I think you ought to know that the woman in your room is really a most notorious prostitute known all down Pennsylvania Avenue as such. For the sake of your own career and reputation I tell you this." The Senator snorted, "Notorious, you say? Why, I had no idea! I'll discharge her in the morning."

Despite my membership in the Hideaway Club, which is not really a club at all, and my warm feelings toward so many of my colleagues, I'm not a very social fellow. Not only in my private hours, but as a legislator also I have always been a loner. I believe any legislator has the obligation to listen to his colleagues and his constituents, hear them out, but then make judgments which are purely his own, based on a rational consideration of the facts involved. I have always voted as though I would never be up for election again, even when I knew I was going to run. Strangely enough, whatever popularity I have been able to achieve I believe I owe to my independence, not capitulation to popular opinion.

In the Senate Chamber the hundred members of the "club" conduct their business at desks arranged in four semi-circles facing a mahogany desk placed on a rostrum at the north end of the chamber. In this spacious setting, with its background of cream and dark red marble and walls of gold silk damask, they address the President of the Senate—officially, the Vice-President of the United States. The Republicans are seated on the Vice-President's left and the Democrats on his right (perhaps to confound popular symbolism). In front of the Vice-President's desk is another long one of marble where the Senate's chief clerk, legislative clerk, parliamentarian and general clerk are located. Two long mahogany tables below the rostrum are for the official reporters who take notes on all that is said. Circling the room is a gallery for the press and visitors.

One of the first things I noticed in the Senate Chamber was that Richard Nixon was scarcely ever to be seen presiding over the Senate, which was his duty as Vice-President. As a matter of fact, shortly after you become a Senator it is your turn to preside. It's a strange feeling to sit up there looking down on men who make the laws. However, when you've done it enough times the thrill departs and the speeches seem to get progressively longer, a thing which never happens when you have the floor. Just to entertain myself I started bringing in a stopwatch to keep track of Nixon's time and mine. He had spent only some twenty hours presiding when I had accumulated more than a hundred. But then, I wasn't out campaigning for nomination as President.

On January 28, 1959, I rose from my mahogany desk in this august chamber to make my maiden speech, as it is embarrassingly called. I had worked on it quite a bit, passed it around the office for suggestions and polished it until it seemed to me every word was shining like a new-minted coin. There was a time when a new Senator was expected to keep quiet for a year—or even two. "Junior" Senators, especially, no matter what their age, are expected to be seen and not heard. Although this tradition has fallen into decay, the delivery of a Senator's "maiden" address is still something of an occasion. All your colleagues come to hear you.

The topic I had chosen was the 10 percent excise tax on telephone calls. It seemed to me that with the war over for so many years it was no longer fair to classify telephones as a luxury. In any case, to my mind excise taxes are regressive and should be repealed.

"Mr. President," I said, "the American people should resent paying each month a 10 percent telephone excise tax as telephone users. In 1941, while I was serving my third term as Congressman-at-large from Ohio, the tax was raised as a war-time measure to meet the threat of aggression from Adolf Hitler's Germany. I have always been opposed to this excise or sales tax, which places a heavy burden on persons making telephone calls. Telephone service is certainly a household as well as a business necessity. . . . Let's eliminate unfair, unfounded and atrocious exicse taxes, such as the tax to which I have specifically referred today."

This address had an immediate and stunning effect on my fellow lawmakers. Nobody even introduced a bill to back me up. The tax persists.

Members of Congress are not required to reveal their stock holdings, but shortly after taking office I prepared to disclose my financial holdings in a letter to the secretary of the Senate, Felton M. Johnson. I listed all my property, including stocks I owned. This list included stock in thirteen oil companies, the Monsanto Chemical Company, Radio Corporation of America, W. R. Grace and Company, and United Fruit Company. I have since then brought the public up to date several times on this matter. I certainly think it is a good way to avoid the kind of conflicting interests which embarrassed my predecessor, Senator Bricker. Indeed, I disposed of my holdings in Pan American World Airways and South Puerto Rico and other sugar companies, which I thought would hamper my work in the Aeronautical and Space Sciences and Agriculture and Forestry Committees.

My decision to declare my assets proved a good break for my wife. She was visiting in Key West, Florida, for a time. She said she was down to her last $8.00 and asked the manager of the motel where she was staying if he would cash her check. He demanded identification. When she told him who she was, he said, "That's all right, I just saw your husband's name on the front page of the Miami *Herald*. It says his net worth is $270,000. I think we can take your check."

About four months after we moved into Senator Bricker's old office I was offered new quarters in the New Senate Office Building. I went over to look at them and decided against the move. The building was up to date, all right, but a committee of nine Senators had stood over the architect and evidently shattered his nerves, and it was appropriately appreciated by headline writers as the "new SOB." There were clocks in it with hands so heavy they shuddered to a stop at a quarter before the hour. There were mail chutes that threatened to take your hand along with your letter. The troubled architect, J. George Stewart, appointed by Eisenhower to coordinate building design and Capitol Hill instructions, tried to explain everything away by saying the bugs weren't out of the building yet—in spite of an expenditure of thirty million dollars, including a million dollars merely for luxurious appointments and fittings. Thirty-seven offices were occupied by Senators whose seniority exceeded mine. After taking a look at the three remaining vacant offices available to me, I went hastily away from there, taking care not to slip and fall on the shiny tile floors which had already caused the hospitalization of two stenographers. I chose a suite on the fourth floor of the old building, including reception room and six offices, and have occupied them happily ever since. The clocks may be old but they work, the walls are thick and solid and the carpeting is safe as well as dignified.

At one time, though, our building was threatened by a rambunctious group of starlings. The starlings became such a nuisance that Capitol workmen went to the length of installing wires charged with electric current on the roofs, window ledges and other projecting surfaces of the building. The electric charge did not kill the starlings, but it jolted them out of their complacency with the result that these birds by the thousands deserted the Capitol for the new Supreme Court building. The Supreme Court blamed Congress and set up a system of electrified wires to deliver shock treatments to the birds. But, while the Justices were chuckling wickedly over the thought that we Senators would be harassed once again by the pestiferous birds, the starlings changed course, made a flight over the Senate Building, and were next seen on Pennsylvania Avenue covering the sides and roof of the Occidental Restaurant.

On February 16, 1959, I delivered my second speech in the Senate. It got a little more attention than my maiden effort, for it was an all-out attack on our civil defense program.

CHAPTER 5

There were three issues of particular concern to me, and all three have evoked some uncivil language. These are civil defense, civil rights and civil liberties.

Not long after I took the oath of office as a Senator I became aggrieved over the way the civil defense was being handled. The defense of civilians in time of war is extremely important—too important, I thought, for political hacks to be in charge of it. I said, "This is a major factor in the defense of our country and in time of national emergency the armed forces take over anyway. It should be the responsibility of our armed forces. States and cities should no longer be permitted to waste taxpayers' money on futile and foolish civil defense programs." On February 16, 1959, I called the attention of my colleagues on the Senate floor to an article in the Cincinnati *Post,* claiming that "tucked away in President Eisenhower's new budget is a request for a big expansion of the civil defense program." I asserted that over the years there had been tremendous unnecessary spending for civil defense. I said that our civil defense program was outmoded and obsolete and it would be a shameful waste of public money to continue in the same pattern. I pointed out that Soviet intercontinental ballistic missiles would soon be spanning continents in twenty minutes, that the Director of Civil Defense would have about twenty minutes to warn the nation, that fast nuclear-hydrogen warheads would kill thousands and radiation thousands more. It seemed to me, I said, that the target of enemy intercontinental missiles would not be Columbus, Ohio, where one of the best buildings in the city had been pre-empted for civil defense headquarters, or Washington, or any key industrial centers, but rather our own missile bases, our retaliatory potential. Were our missile bases to be wiped out, any war would be over as soon as it started. On the other hand, these bases of ours are widely dispersed and some are hidden deep enough to be impervious to attack. I pleaded that we stop wasting the time and effort of good patriotic citizens who had volunteered for civil defense work.

At that time, after a two-year study in Washington, the Civil Defense Agency had published and distributed 850,000 copies of a guidebook for residents within twenty miles of the Washington Monument. The book's purpose was to show evacuation escape routes to cities in Maryland, Virginia and West Virginia. The book gave instructions on how to build basement shelters and how to build up food supplies for a two-week period. All this seemed to me to reassure our citizens in an area where no reassurance was justified and to encourage anti-social attitudes. I was shocked at stories of shelter builders who had put in, along with their food supplies, a stock of rifles and ammunition to keep their neighbors out. In all this there was grave danger that, coasting along in the comfort of false security, people might entertain the idea that they could *escape* the consequences of nuclear attack. Surely such attitudes would weaken our national resolve to work toward the more difficult and less easily attainable goal of permanent peace in our time.

I was the first member of the United States Senate to speak out on this subject. I wrote articles about it for the *Saturday Evening Post, The Progressive, True* magazine, and my own newsletter, "Straight from Washington." The more I studied the huge amounts spent since World War II on civil defense, the more irritated I became. Since much legislation is done by unanimous consent, I took to staying doggedly at my post in the Senate Chamber when appropriations were up for civil defense expenditures. One Senator alone can save the government money when he puts his mind to it.

Gradually, people lined up to support me. If ever I felt sure of myself about a subject, it was this one. I studied everything I could find and during trips to England and Europe I made inquiries about what was being done. I soon learned that in Canada, England, France, Italy, West Germany and other countries little or no money was being spent on civil defense. There was nothing comparable to the huge expenditures involved in the civil defense boondoggle in the United States. The federal government was spending more than 120,000 dollars a day on the defense of civilians in case of war, in an atmosphere of poor planning, confused thinking and colossal ineptitude. About 60 percent was being assigned for political reasons, some for political hacks and defeated office-holders for whom the Office of Civil Defense Mobilization also provided a cozy haven. More than 40 percent of the personnel of this agency drew salaries of 10,000 dollars a year or more. Much of the money was wrung from taxpayers and went into the building of shelters at the expense of constructive building programs for schools, hospitals and housing.

In Ohio, we started an audit of surplus property worth almost two million dollars, which had been donated to civil defense programs in the course of a few years. Much of the property couldn't even be located. The audit turned up barber kits, shaving kits, garbage cans and a thousand gimcracks of absolute worthlessness "in case of emergency." Much of the equipment, from typewriters to adding machines had, by some strange process, wound up in the homes of local civil defense administrators. Other Senators reported similar waste of funds in their home cities. But it seemed to

71

me that Ohio provided all the examples you could need to convince any sane man that money was being thrown away. In my state more than 100,000 dollars' worth of penicillin had to be destroyed because it was found unacceptable by the Food and Drug Administration.

In Columbus, Ohio, funds had been put into a traffic light control system which was supposed to make it easier to evacuate the area in case of nuclear attack. The manual for this electronic evacuation weighed nearly five pounds. Freely translated, it told any resident with enough time on his hands to go through it that, in case of nuclear attack, he should get in his car and leave town the fastest way open to him.

One civil defense directive, promulgated by some lame-brain officer, had a sentence which read as follows: "All funeral coaches must pull to the curb and stop when the siren sounds, although the occupants are not required to seek shelter."

Recently I saw a movie called "Ladybug, Ladybug," which shows the panic and distress caused in a suburban community when the children in a public school are led to believe that a real enemy attack is imminent. The movie didn't take any strong stand on our fallout shelter program, but it did bring home how unendurable life would be in one of them, even for a short time, even with all the gadgets and packaged foods you could install. Add to that the fact that the conditions of modern warfare make these shelters completely useless—if we were attacked by missiles armed with hydrogen warheads the effects would last not for months, but probably for years—and you begin to wonder why our money cannot be spent to keep the streets of our cities safe for the demands of peacetime, rather than to construct futile holes in the ground.

If I am wrong, why is it I have never encountered a civil defense official in my own state who has built one of these shelters for himself?

72

One of the reactions that pleased me most in my campaign against the civil defense boondoggle came from Lyndon Johnson. He has credited me with saving taxpayers fifteen million dollars in reduced appropriations for this purpose. This was in connection with a request for unanimous consent to agree to a civil defense appropriation measure. I remained in the Senate Chamber over some days. I repeatedly objected until the whole thing was dropped.

It long seemed to me that the armed forces ought to take over the question of civil defense which is, after all, an important part of the defense of our country. This was done soon after President Kennedy took office. I believe our tremendous power for retaliation is the only power we have—that and the gradual lessening of cold war tensions which the late President worked so hard to bring about. Others have apparently come around to this point of view, since the Senate in 1964 refused to authorize the $380 million appropriations for fallout shelters which the House had previously authorized.

As for civil liberties, I had taken for granted, perhaps naively, that all sane Americans are in favor of these. Ever since I read the Bill of Rights in a public school textbook, I had found the antics of men like Senator Joseph McCarthy virtually incredible. I think he did more to aid Communism abroad than any other American of our time, every time he opened his mouth.

I remember one time when I was speaking before a hostile, pro-McCarthy audience a fellow stood up and defied me to name "one innocent person" who had been injured by McCarthy's allegations. "Name one!" I cried, "I will name 18,787 employees of the State Department of the United States."

At the time I became a Senator I was under the impression

that the worst excesses of the McCarthy period were safely in the past and that America had repudiated his methods of terrorism, name-calling and wholesale blackmail. I found out I was a little ahead of myself on this score.

In November 1959 I received an invitation to be guest speaker at a civil rights banquet in New York City. As it happened, Senator Langer had spoken there a year or so before. Then on December 9 I received a release, dated December 3, signed by a man named Neil E. Wetterman, Americanism chairman, Hamilton County Council of the American Legion of Ohio. The statement expressed disapproval and censored "the Honorable Stephen M. Young for his scheduled appearance as guest speaker." The resolution stated, "the Hamilton County Council also questions the propriety of Senator Young's forthcoming attendance in according this infamous group the prestige of his position as a United States Senator. We strongly urge the Senator from Ohio to reconsider and withdraw from such participation so as not to become a tool of the Communist apparatus." This insulting action caused me to write Wetterman:

"Sir:

"So—you self-appointed censors and self-proclaimed super-duper 100 percent America Firsters censure me. You professional veterans who proclaim your vainglorious chauvinism have the effrontery to issue a press release gratuitously offering an expression of censure and making urgent demand that I cancel a speaking engagement previously made.

"I repudiate your resolution, Buster, and your pompous, self-righteous, holier-than-thou title of 'Americanism Chairman.' Why don't you read and try to understand that cornerstone of our liberties, the Constitution of the United States?

"If, in your press release, you asserted, or implied that

I am likely to become a tool of the Communist apparatus, you are a liar.

"Another thing—why don't you puffed up patriots write my American Legion Post demanding my expulsion? Or, do you self-appointed vigilantes demand that I submit a list of speaking engagements for clearance by your outfit before I, as a Senator of the United States, open my mouth in public?"

I telephoned the Department of Justice regarding the Emergency Civil Liberties Committee. Here is the telegram I got from J. Walter Yeagley, Assistant Attorney General of the United States:

CONCERNING YOUR INQUIRY EMERGENCY CIVIL RIGHTS COMMITTEE. THIS COMMITTEE IS NOT ON THE ATTORNEY GENERAL'S LIST.

The Hamilton County Council of the American Legion took up the challenge. They threatened to expel me. I paid them no mind. On the evening of Tuesday, December 15, 1960, I was scheduled to speak at the Civil Liberties Union affair which, as it happened, was to be a celebration of the 169th anniversary of the Bill of Rights.

When Monday, December 14, came around, I was afflicted with such a severe cold and experienced so much difficulty in speaking, I would have canceled almost any other engagement. I made up my mind I would keep this one, even if I had to help celebrate the 169th anniversary of the Bill of Rights from a stretcher.

At the dinner I blasted both Communists and Fascists, as well as the super-duper patriots who had already started to make trouble through their ultra-right wing organizations.

"I will speak," I said, "wherever I please. In fact, I would enjoy addressing a meeting of the National Association of Manufacturers or the United States Chamber of Commerce, many of whose directors are Fascist-minded and who, in my judgment, seek to crush labor unions, weaken the right of collective bargaining, and are now trying to impose a federal sales tax across the board—and, at the same time, try to reduce income taxes. . . . Civil liberties is freedom to think and freedom to express one's views—rights that people everywhere are entitled to enjoy, whether they are Americans, Chinese, Russians, or people living anywhere in the world."

I pleaded with my audience to repudiate the fear-mongers. I also lashed out against Communism. In fact, in that speech I denounced Communism thirteen times.

Result? The fourth Ohio district of the American Legion, which covers twenty chapters, again asked for my expulsion. Mr. Wetterman said they wanted me out on "grounds of disloyalty, negligence of duty, and conduct unbecoming to a Legionnaire."

Editorial comment all over the country came to my defense. Said the New York *Herald Tribune*, "Whatever other significance may be found in this little episode, it means that a United States Senator has spoken out sharply for the right of a citizen to speak his mind to whom he pleases and when he pleases, and if the Bill of Rights means anything, it certainly means that."

On June 17th of that year, I praised a New York schoolboy for turning down an American Legion Citizenry award. The Legion's William Longuet, post commander where this incident occurred, told the boy the action was "a lifetime mistake that will blacken you forever."

I told reporters I considered the post commander a "self-appointed *Gauleiter,* or a creature with long furry ears." Stephen Payne, the seventeen-year-old senior who refused the award, had astounded and shocked his thousand classmates in Westbury, Long Island. But I praised him for his "independence of thought and demonstration of courage in refusing to accept a citizenry award from an organization you had concluded you did not respect . . ."

Wetterman and a few of his associates who were playing God with other people's patriotism really tried hard to have me thrown out of the American Legion. They had a resolution introduced in the Department of Ohio, to which I paid no attention. Evidently the delegates either shelved it or defeated it. I am still listed as a member of the American Legion and some months ago addressed a Legion meeting and was well received.

Speaking of the Fascist-minded, one of the most disturbing phenomena of recent years has been the rise in power and reputation of the so-called ultra- or radical right wing. During my half-century in politics I have known many varieties of rightist radicals and fought them—in Ohio and in Congress. Today they are better financed, stronger and more successful than ever before. In April 1961, I stood up on the floor of the Senate and said that in my judgment the John Birch Society and others like it are as serious a threat to our security and our way of life as internal Communists. In a *Saturday Evening Post* article less than a year later I found it necessary to go even further and to declare the radical right a *more* serious threat to our democratic traditions than are the American admirers of Communism.

I believe that even the assassination of President Kennedy has done little to shock the fear-mongers and hate-mongers out of their lunacy. American Communists may have tried to infiltrate our schools, our political parties, our mass media, our entertainment and labor unions to further their cause, but they didn't get anywhere.

The ultra-rightists, on the other hand, have tried to destroy all our civil liberties, undermine the institutions which are our freedom, and even to wreck our Supreme Court and to repudiate the United Nations, which is our principal hope

77

for avoiding war in our time. Today they are more on the rise than on the wane. They want to wreck our program of foreign aid, blind to the consequences. While denying that they are anti-Semitic, they proceed in underhanded ways to vilify the foreign born and members of minorities. They breed confusion and suspicion. They are the best friends the Communists ever had because all they really accomplish is to sow distrust and disaffection among our friends in other lands and to cast doubts on our integrity and our sanity as a country. They operate under all sorts of names, from the John Birch Society to the Christian Anti-Communist crowd, or the American Council of Christian Laymen. Each group claims to be functioning independently of the others, but the ring-leaders make up a closely-knit fraternity, and their tactics are all the same—smears, lies, vigilantism, contempt for law and justice. If they can't impeach the Chief Justice of the United States, they will settle for a school teacher in Maine, a clergyman in California. They are pleased at any opportunity to create discord, whether it is to impede the fluoridation of our water (which they consider a Communist plot because, as they put it, "Fluoride weakens the mind and induces docility"), to persuade a school library to censor books—or claim, as did the Congress of Freedom, a federation of rightist groups, that "foreigners are running the country and the best way to get rid of all our problems would be to kill all the damn niggers and Jews." They constitute a definite danger to our civil liberties for the simple reason that they are taken seriously by so many. It is difficult to understand how any adult in possession of his mental faculties could possibly call former President Eisenhower a conscious agent of Communist conspiracy, or seriously demand the impeachment of Chief Justice Earl Warren. Sensible people know that the Communist threat is real and dangerous to our American way of life but that it comes from the Soviet

Union and Red China, not from the Supreme Court of the United States. We Americans may not always agree with its decisions, but we should agree that this Court deserves our respect. Ours is a government of law and not of men.

The man who invented the roller coaster was a good judge of human characteristics. He figured that people like being scared to death. He must have been an ancestor—grandfather, perhaps—of Robert Welch, Jr., founder and *fuehrer* of the John Birch Society. The Birch Society has formalized such a sophisticated structure that it rivals the syndication of the Communists. Because Robert Welch and his colleagues have money and influence to pour into the organization, they are able to attract thousands of members. When Attorney General Robert Kennedy says, as he did a few years ago, "I think they are ridiculous and I don't think anybody should pay too much attention to them," I think he underestimates them. They would like to be underestimated while they gather their forces among the ignorant, the gullible and the disgruntled.

I don't think we should send around Congressional committees conducting investigations into their activities. We have had enough of that. I *do* think that we must vehemently defend the rights of our neighbors to hold their own views and to speak up about them. It is in this belief that I have fought the radical right-wing in Senate speeches and articles, as well as in my correspondence.

It is the atmosphere of hatred, suspicion and violence engendered by extremist groups of this kind which has led to the sort of lawlessness and insanity which culminated in the assassination of our late great President, John F. Kennedy. Yet, in the winter of 1963, the John Birch Society brazenly placed a full-page ad in the Sunday New York *Times* of December 15th calling the assassination of President Kennedy the result of a Communist conspiracy. In the larger sense,

I say his death could be laid more closely to the door of the Birch Society itself, for it is they who have done much to whip up the spirit of violence and suspicion in our land.

Senator Kuchel, Assistant Minority Leader of the Senate, who was assailed by the right-wing John Birch Society which urged the impeachment of Chief Justice Warren and the defeat of Senator Kuchel in his bid for re-election, countered with his own proposal. Senator Kuchel, who has acquired a fine reputation for intelligent voting and competence, proposed organizing a "Sons of Birches" society. Another Senator then suggested that either society could well have as its motto: "Drive dangerously—the pedestrian you kill may be a Communist."

When it comes to civil rights, I believe we are dealing with the most important domestic issue of our times. The first time I ever encountered the problem of race prejudice was when I was a boy in Norwalk. I used to play ball with a Negro boy named Ham Easy. We were on the same football team in school. Then some people complained to my father that I was associating with a Negro. My father was shocked not at the friendship, but at their bigotry. I was, too, and I have never recovered from it.

My law partner of many years was Jewish. I have found every allegation against minority groups, whether in respect to their intelligence, personality, loyalty or abilities, to be 100 percent false. In Ohio, for as long as I can remember, Negroes have been able to go to any hotel and sit in the main dining room.

The thing is, I believe even legislation for Negro rights is not enough, although I am sponsor of three civil rights bills. We must educate ourselves to overcome deep-rooted attitudes of ignorance, prejudice and hostility. We have to learn in our hearts that we are all created equal—and I don't mean separate but equal.

Meanwhile, legislation is absolutely necessary. The role of the Southern Senators in this fight is largely destructive for the filibuster can never be anything but a negative and divisive technique. No less than eighteen of our Senators from the Deep South today are fine men, outstanding Senators, but they have this blind spot. They are like victims of brainwashing. Their prejudices go to the quick and even when they don't—and surely President Johnson is a memorable example of the fact that a Southerner does not have to be a bigot—they are afraid of their constituents. There are many who feel that Richard Russell, the senior Senator from Georgia, would have been Democratic nominee for President of the United States except for the fact that he was born in Georgia. It seems unfortunate so many capable Southern legislators are forced to maintain rigid anti-civil rights positions to survive politically. Let us hope that in a few years this present struggle for civil rights will be behind us and that really great public servants like Richard Russell, Harry Byrd, Russell Long, Herman Talmadge, J. William Fulbright, Jim Pearson, Paul Douglas, and Sam Ervin, to name only a few, will find no prejudice whatever against them at any place throughout this broad land simply because they were born in a state that was a part of the Old Confederacy.

In the fall of 1963 I called for twenty-four-hour sessions in the Senate, if necessary. Some of my colleagues thought this might put an exhausting burden on those of us who are up in years. I replied, "The magnitude of the problem does not justify this excuse for abandoning the fight for meaningful civil rights legislation. We who favor the President's proposal will protect any colleagues who have various reasons why they cannot suffer the hardships that will be involved in

81

breaking a possible filibuster." The Toledo *Blade,* one of Ohio's greatest newspapers, slapped me on the back admiringly in an editorial the following day:

"Does that sound like a seventy-four-year-old Senator," they asked, "weary of office, short of stamina and long on tired blood? Nope, it sounds suspiciously like an indefatigable incumbent who wants to make it very plain that he's got the moxie needed to become what is generally called a vigorous candidate for re-election."

I believe in unlimited debate in the Senate. Perhaps the present rule of cloture which calls for a two-thirds majority of those Senators present and voting should be reduced to three-fifths. I would support such a liberalization of the Senate rules. Whether or not the Senate would be wise to provide cloture by majority vote is something else again; I have grave doubts that a mere majority of Senators present and voting should be permitted to close debates. I believe we must zealously safeguard the rights of minorities in the Senate and elsewhere. Public opinion, while often correct, has never been considered a sound principle in the administration of justice; two thousand years ago the crowd in the market place cried, "Crucify him, crucify him!" and the greatest judge who ever trod on this earth was crucified between two thieves.

Senators may judge a man unfit to serve as colleague and compel him to stand aside. If Governor Ross Barnett of Mississippi uses his white supremacy tactics to run for the Senate in 1964, I believe this man, who flouted the law of our country and was guilty of inciting mob violence leading to two deaths and serious injuries to twenty-nine deputy United States marshals, should be barred by the Senate. In 1947 the Senate barred its door to Theodore Bilbo, who had been elected in Mississippi. In fact, a Republican Senator, none other than the late Robert A. Taft of Ohio, was one of those who demanded that Bilbo stand aside.

It is my firm belief that no matter what tactics my Southern colleagues use, before very long they will have to come to grips with the fact that true equality for the Negro in this land is a hundred years overdue. They will have to submit to the advance of progress.

Early in July 1963, Washington newspapers headlined that plans were under way for a massive civil rights march on Washington and that demonstrators would stage sit-ins in offices of Senators and Representatives until civil rights legislation was enacted into law. Wayne Hays, Congressman from Ohio's Eighteenth District, and some other Congressional colleagues said that if such a thing occurred they would close their offices and excuse their employees until the demonstrators had left Washington. On July 11th I made a speech on the floor of Congress pointing out that my office belonged to the ten million citizens of Ohio, and I would not allow the Senatorial business of my state to be disrupted by demonstrators crowding into my room or any of the offices I occupy, or permit members of my staff to be intimidated.

"The legal right of citizens to march on Washington to influence a Senator is clear," I said. "Citizens have a right to petition and to lobby. However, a mass invasion and demonstration is unwise and is a disorderly way to dramatize any cause." I stated, "I will not be coerced or pushed around by ten or a thousand demonstrators, nor will I close my office and deprive Ohio schoolchildren and parents and other constituents of the opportunity to be served by my staff members and me. If a large number of men and women crowd into the office I occupy threatening to remain until the Senate does something or other responsive to their demand, I will personally and forcibly eject them, if necessary. If I am banged around in the process, I accept that as an occupational hazard."

As it turned out, the freedom march on Washington was one of the most orderly and dignified demonstrations for a cause in the history of man's struggle for freedom and equality. My concern proved needless, but the principle remains. As Congressman-at-large in the thirties, I handled for the Administration the introduction in the House of Representatives of the first anti-poll tax bill that was ever passed. At that time the Senate smothered it in committee. That is why I was eager to co-sponsor all three of the civil rights bills before Congress, and did so.

Another aspect of civil rights is religious liberty. I believe that the Supreme Court's decision on prayer was altogether in the spirit of the Bill of Rights, which spells this question out most carefully. I think that emotional attempts to accuse the Court of anti-religious feeling because prayers cannot be recited in public schools beclouds the point of the law— the safeguarding of the concept of separation of church and state.

Regarding the most recent Supreme Court decision concerning prayers in public schools, I have studied briefs filed by both sides, and the decision. I have, of course, carefully read some news accounts and editorial comments. There is no alternative to accepting in good spirit and good faith the Supreme Court's decision that our Constitution prohibits official prayers in the public schools.

The First Amendment to our Constitution states, "Congress shall make no law respecting an establishment of religion or prohibiting the free exercise thereof."

This same prohibition is fastened on the states by the 14th Amendment. This recent Supreme Court decision was by a vote of eight to one, with Associate Justice Potter Stewart dissenting. I find it difficult to conceive of any change in the First Amendment which would not erode the principle and purpose for which it was written into the Bill of Rights.

To keep church out of the state and to keep the state out of the church is to guarantee absolute freedom of religious worship without giving special favor to one religion over others or even equal favors to all religions. Although we may disagree with decisions of our Supreme Court, it is important for Americans to maintain the Constitutional principle of support of such decisions. Our Supreme Court has the duty and responsibility to interpret the laws of our country.

Justice Clark in the majority opinion said, "The place of religion in our society is an exalted one, achieved through a long tradition of reliance on the home, the church, and the inviolable citadel of the individual heart and mind. We have come to recognize through bitter experience that it is not within the power of government to invade that citadel, whether its purpose or effect be to aid or oppose, to advance or retard."

The Washington *Post* editorially stated, "Once more the Supreme Court has ruled that government in the United States may not intrude its power into the realm of religion. Rightly read, this decision must be recognized not as a prohibition of prayer but as a protection of prayer. Religion as a vital element in American evolution and culture is strengthened, not weakened, by the Court's strictures on required religious observances in the public schools."

Despite my strong convictions in all these matters, I have never been able to rival my Southern colleagues when it came to occupying the Senate floor in long speeches. One of the longest speeches I ever made lasted less than an hour— and that speech was against the civil defense program. On one other occasion I spoke for two hours in behalf of civil rights. But the strong stands I have taken as a Senator have not been met with an attitude of impartial silence on the part of my constituents. They write me letters.

CHAPTER 6

✍ *I have never thought of myself as any kind of model letter writer like Lord Chesterfield or Madame de Sévigné. Any fame that would have been mine I hoped would come through my speeches on the floor of Congress or the stands I have taken on crucial legislation, certainly not through my correspondence. True, I have always admired succinctness in communication, and for that reason have treasured a postcard I got shortly after I voted against a bonus for veterans of World War I back in 1933. It said:*

"DEAR CONGRESSMAN:
  "*My dog left home when he heard I had voted for you.*"

As a busy lawyer over the years I made it a rule to try to write briefly and clearly to clients and others. I like to receive letters from Ohio citizens. It benefits me in my work as their public servant to have their views and advice. We try to answer every letter and postcard. Citizens can disagree with their Senator without being uncivil or insulting. In replying to most letter writers who express disagreement, I try to give reasons why my opinion differs from theirs. I try to make these letters cordial but to the point. I feel I have been sent to Washington to serve my state and country with honesty and with dignity. However, there is no requirement that a Senator refrain from defending himself against abuse. If my replies to insulting correspondence have brought me

87

some attention, I suspect the reason is that I have not wasted words; sometimes I have replied in kind, only more so.

I receive from ten to twenty thousand letters every month. I certainly can't read them all unless I abandon the rest of my duties. My staff handles most of the correspondence, but they are under orders to let me see any letter which shows individual thought, effort and attention to the issues, whether the writer agrees with me or not. I have also asked to be shown aggressively abusive letters, which has involved me in a kind of epistolary crusade.

I began composing one-line answers to objectionable letters shortly after I took the oath of office. I had never thought of releasing them to the newspapers or even mentioning them until one day Lowell Bridwell of Scripps-Howard asked if he could see some of the correspondence. My assistant, Herb Jolovitz, turned over a few samples to him. Soon magazines like the *Saturday Evening Post, The Reporter, Time* and *Look* were publishing articles quoting my correspondence. After a while the demand began to exceed the supply. Obviously short letters save time, a fact not fully appreciated by all my correspondents. One citizen, for instance, sent in a very long letter stuffed with disparaging remarks on labor unions, a strong expression that minimum wage laws should be repealed, that price controls for farmers were outrageous, and with angry comments about welfare programs and Chief Justice Earl Warren. I think the answer I sent off on that occasion is appropriate:

"DEAR SIR:
"What else is new?"

I remember this particular constituent because he later wrote:

"Please reconsider your decision not to run for re-election. I would thoroughly and completely enjoy the pleasure of campaigning against you."

88

So, on December 24, 1963, I announced that I would seek a second term as Senator from Ohio. As I told a Washington reporter several years ago, I don't think you have to believe the customer is always right to get elected—I have not softened the tone of my answers to crackpots since I've decided to run again.

Every man has the right to answer back when he is being bullied. And so, when some wiseacre challenges my sincerity or patriotism, I let him have it. I especially refuse to take abuse from self-appointed vigilantes who try to play God with another man's patriotism.

A fellow in Cincinnati sent me a long tirade complaining about my behavior in Congress and out of it. He went on and on. I answered him:

"SIR:

"*No, I don't believe I have long furry ears. I do thank you, however, for your gentlemanly manner of calling me a jackass.*"

There was really nothing to tell the man in South Euclid who said I was the sort of fellow who would enjoy desecrating the graves in Arlington Cemetery except:

"SIR:

"*You are a liar.*"

That is what I did write, and I would be delighted to tell him so to his face any time.

From the president of a pharmaceutical company came a letter of four single-spaced pages explaining why I should accept an appointment as honorary director of their board. The letter was most persuasive, citing, among other things, the Greek legend of the giant Antaeus and comparing him to big business. There were quotations in French from Lamartine, several sentences in faultless Latin and some mighty words from the pages of Victor Hugo, all marshaled in this remarkable document to persuade me that, unless I joined a certain industrial organization in Massachusetts as a board director without further delay, "future generations" would suffer dire consequences for my refusal. Despite these warnings I felt constrained to write back:

"My answer regarding your offer of appointment is no."

They have ceased to bother me.

A Cleveland doctor accused me of favoring socialized medicine because I supported Medicare. I replied:

"You have been entirely misinformed. In fact, you have been duped."

To a Kettering, Ohio, man of like mind I wrote:

"I am sending you a letter received this morning, evidently from some crackpot who used your name."

One of these anti-Medicare constituents displayed such startling ignorance of the plan I thought it would be kind to take more space than usual. On that occasion I wrote:

"I unhesitatingly assert you have not read the bill, you have not read any committee hearings and reports relating to surgical and medical care of the elderly. You have probably been impressed by some pamphlet or book received from one of your insurance companies. . . . I will cast my vote in accord with my study, my information and my conscience."

The Kettering correspondent had been even more insulting than his fellow crackbrains. He had written on the margin of his letter, "Be a man." If he had come right up to me and said that, he would have received not a written answer but a punch in the jaw.

Another hater of Medicare accused the Kennedys of conducting "drunken parties in our White House," and "spending millions to keep one colored man in a college where he is not wanted." I wrote this Akron woman that she ought to be ashamed of writing such insulting and libelous statements when she had no facts to back them up. I doubt if it did any good in her case, but *I* felt a little better.

One nasty item in my mail protested that Mrs. John F. Kennedy had been presented with a horse by the President of Pakistan, and this horse was transported free by the Air Force. "I require that you procure a horse for me and have it brought to me in the same manner," I replied:

"DEAR SIR:

"Acknowledging your letter wherein you insult the wife of our President, I am wondering why you need a horse when there is already one jackass at your address."

I tried to stop myself, but ended up by telling an overwrought minister:

"As one Methodist to another may I suggest that you concentrate on preaching the Gospel instead of insulting a public servant."

Another minister criticized my vote against the confirmation of Lewis L. Strauss for Secretary of Commerce under Eisenhower. He said my stand "must have been politically inspired, and as such it stinks." My reply:

"Your insulting letter demonstrates a non-Christian attitude. Possibly you could avoid that in the future if you would study the Gospels and try to learn more about saving souls instead of insulting and untruthfully attacking the motives of public officials."

There have also been letters denouncing men of the cloth as Communists. "Folk like you," was my answer to one of

91

them who claimed that many Protestant ministers are Communists, and who ignore altogether the serious threat against our country coming from Communist Russia and Red China, "are like individuals who hoist their skirts from imaginary mice."

A Mr. B dispatched a postcard from Columbus:

"DEAR SENATOR YOUNG:

"A group of us are beginning a new society here in Columbus. We advocate immediate complete unilateral disarmament. We call ourselves INSANE. Our problem is that we need a leader. Would you like to become president?"

I wrote back that Mr. B obviously had the essential qualifications and should assume the presidency in my place.

This one arrived only recently on the stationery of a Cincinnati insurance company:

"You are doing a great job in selling America down the river. How much more did the Russians pay you to approve the test ban treaty? Fortunately, there are not enough Reds and Pinkos in Ohio to re-elect you, and for that we are all grateful."

I informed this friendly soul (I think, correctly) that:

"You and the leaders of Red China completely agree."

I think my shortest answer to date was to an Oklahoma editor who wanted me to take back everything I had said against the ultra-right wing:

"SIR:

"No."

A lawyer accused me once of underestimating the danger of Communism. I answered:

"Don't give me any more of this unsolicited advice. I know it costs nothing, but that is exactly what it is worth."

92

At the time of the Cuban crisis in October 1962, a fellow in Norwood, Ohio, was moved to write me:

"I assume you and your cohorts are busily engaged in equipping our planes with white flags containing a yellow stripe."

I asked him where he was when John F. Kennedy was in combat in the Pacific, and noted that he was hurling his insults a long distance from Cuba.

A lady in Lima, Ohio never got over the fact that I refused to let Senator Lausche escort me on the day I was sworn in. Perhaps my answer to her will throw light on my point of view:

"My distinguished colleague from Ohio did not choose to support me for election, although I was the Democratic nominee for Senator at that time. If he voted for me it was a well-kept secret . . . not having his support when I was waging a difficult contest against the greatest Republican vote-getter in Ohio. You have a most peculiar mentality indeed to decide that I needed the support of his arm after the citizens of Ohio had elected me by a majority of 155,000. You are 100 percent wrong."

All the way from New Orleans came this masterpiece:

"Dear Senator:

"From sources such as the American Legion news of your confused outbursts have gradually leaked down here in the South and has [sic] caused some comment among my friends.

"It was the consensus that the people of Ohio have evidently made a mistake in electing you to the Senate. However, I disagree as in many cases involving confused minor executives. Sometimes they can be saved.

"It might pay you to have a talk with some of your fellow representatives and possibly your doctor to determine

93

how your mind has become so muddled. The Day of the Liberal is fast drawing to a close and if the present administration doesn't watch its step with the thousands of wild-eyed professors that have been coming into Washington by the trainloads, our great United States might pass into the hands of some of the glib-voiced fiends."

I don't know what you would have told this philosopher, but I hazarded the guess that he was "the south end of a horse headed north" and begged him to remove me from his mailing list.

One Indianapolis man who had criticized my *Saturday Evening Post* article warning of danger on the right, asked me:

"Who do you think you represent?"

I was glad to be able to inform him:

"Buster, I know I don't represent a pipsqueak like you."

I was once urged by a Cuyahoga County constituent to stamp out Little Orphan Annie! Here's a copy of the complaint:

"I am writing about my objections to the comic strip, 'Little Orphan Annie.' It has very definite Communistic leanings. It is an insult to the American public and since it is read by the youth of America, it is spreading Communistic ideas to the young. The language used in the strip on October 22 definitely degraded students. Even though, in the last picture, the Communist is called an 'idiot,' it does not make up for the other six pictures which glorify Communism.

"As a Senator, is there anything that you can do to stop this type of propaganda for Communism?"

So, let's stamp out Little Orphan Annie. Perhaps also *Gone With the Wind* should be removed from bookstores because of Scarlett O'Hara!

A woman once wrote a letter to the Cincinnati *Enquirer* accusing me of making "false and irresponsible statements about Robert Welch and the John Birch Society." It seems I had stated somewhere that Mr. Welch made money as a lawyer, an impression the lady happily corrected by pointing out that the guiding genius of the ultra-right "never passed a bar examination." Her letter also explained that Mr. Welch never kept for himself the money he made from speeches, but turned it over to the society, that neither dues nor contributions to the society are tax exempt (I had never said they were), that the society keeps "careful records" and that "every smear from Senator Young and others is a boost for the pro-American John Birch Society." I wrote to the *Enquirer* correspondent:

"In the interest of fairness, I feel it my duty to send this letter, which was clipped from the Enquirer, *to you and let you know that some crackbrain is using your name for such correspondence. Possibly you will wish to see that adequate measures are taken to protect your good name."*

Sometimes the original correspondence I get is almost as brief as my answers. A Cincinnati lady once wrote:

"DEAR SIR:

"What is wrong about Representative Scherer being a vigilante? It is my humble opinion that you are an old reprobate and a disgrace to the state of Ohio."

I must admit that I thought hard trying to frame an appropriate rejoinder to that one. At last it came to me:

"Lady, reading your abusive, insulting and untruthful letter causes me to feel happy I am not your husband."

Somehow, I can't help feeling that she is going to have the last word.

95

A Columbus citizen wondered how I could possibly favor confirming the appointment of Robert F. Kennedy as Attorney General when I was not even a member of the family. I pointed out that Lieutenant Colonel John Eisenhower served for more than twenty-six months as an aide to his father and was awarded a high Army decoration for distinguished service, while I would not judge Milton Eisenhower's employment during his brother's administration. I assured my correspondent that his letter would be placed "temporarily in my crackpot file and later consigned to the wastebasket."

"When are you going to actively support a measure to withdraw our financial support and membership from the United Nations?"

I answered:

"Never."

I once got this orchid from a constituent:

"In my opinion you are a disgrace to Ohio. We Conservatives will take you like Grant took Richmond."

I even got a telegram one time calling for impeachment of President Kennedy and urging immediate action. My answer began:

"Some crackpot sent me a telegram to which your name was affixed."

One writer was kind enough to concede that I am not "a card-carrying member of the Communist Party," but took pains to inform me that "we are at war with the Communist bloc whether you realize it or not." He offered "best wishes for an early end to your Senate term . . ." I hope I may be excused for calling him "so ignorant that if a blackbird had your brains he would fly backwards."

96

From Fairfield County came this letter:

"You New Deal spenders—spend and spend, tax and tax—you sicken me. Let's return to rugged individualism. I stand on my own two feet, don't ask any favors from Washington, am against creeping socialism, against handouts and aid for the aged."

This, from a constituent who enjoyed the federal school lunch program in public school, received educational training as a GI, college education under the GI Bill of Rights, bought his farm with an FHA loan, enjoyed checks from the Eisenhower Soil Bank Program for not raising crops, and farm supports to help him receive more for his farm products. Incidentally, his father and mother are receiving social security checks each month.

If a Senator allows himself to be governed by the opinions of his constituents at home, however devoted he may be to them or they to him, he throws away all the rich results of previous experience and study and simply becomes a commonplace exponent of popular sentiments which may change in a few days.

Such a course will degrade any man's statesmanship. A Senator's vote on that basis would be simply an echo of current opinion. It would certainly not be the result of honest, mature deliberation.

What would you say if you opened the morning mail and found a treasure like this:

"Buster, you represent the epitomy [sic] of pigsty thinking and cattle-type action.

"Obviously, dialectics is something that is beyond your short grasp. For instance, before you commence with your diurnal diarrhea of the mouth why do not for a change get the facts and attempt for once to make a truthful statement?"

97

I studied this masterpiece of English prose carefully and replied with a question:

"*Are you sure, Buster, or Junior, that you are able to think?*"

I agree with Edmund Burke that there is "a limit to which forebearance ceases to be a virtue."

Not more than five or ten of the letters I receive every month are abusive. Some are extremely kind and flattering. On March 17, 1960, I opened my mail and found this one:

"DEAR STEPHEN:

"*I have always heard of your reputation for courage and I saw it amply displayed on the floor two days ago and then yesterday and I congratulate you. Courage is something lacking in America today and to find it so obviously displayed in one of my colleagues is a reassuring experience. With all best wishes.*"

The letter was signed Barry Goldwater.

CHAPTER 7

Whenever I think of my arrival in Washington in 1959 I seem to recall the white monuments as being paler than they had been, as if they were still suffering from the aftereffects of acute McCarthyism. Under President Eisenhower, Washington seemed to slumber in a somnolent air of timidity and restraint. Generals, I guess, are only brave on the battlefield. When it came to doing anything constructive about housing, education, economy or any legislation, all you ever heard from President Eisenhower was a confusion of ill-chosen words which added up to nothing. As a result, if you listened quietly on a spring afternoon, a sound like a soft political snore seemed to rise from the Potomac and engulf the area in a kind of socio-political smog.

My good friend, the late Sam Rayburn, Speaker of the House of Representatives, once said, "President Eisenhower is a good man. He was born in my Congressional district. Everyone in Denison, Texas, says he was a good baby. However, he moved to Kansas and when he was sixty years old he decided he was a Republican." It was typical of Eisenhower's vision and ability to make value judgments that he dismissed the launching of the first satellite into outer space by the Soviets as "that basketball in the sky." I hope in the lifetime of my granddaughters no professional soldier is ever again President of the United States.

President Kennedy suffered much agony and embarrassment over the ill-fated invasion of the Bay of Pigs in 1961, but he was merely being confronted with the chickens that had hatched from eggs laid during the Eisenhower administration.

In 1960, when Castro first seized the property of Americans in Cuba, we simply withdrew our ambassador. It was easy after the Bay of Pigs tragedy for armchair interventionists to say that we should have thrown in our air power. But these men tend to think of other human beings as ciphers, not flesh-and-blood people. It evidently means nothing to them that thousands of Cuban men and women and children would have been killed and many Americans as well, not to mention the international consequences of such highhanded tactics.

I still feel my ears turning pink with embarrassment for this country whenever I think about the U-2 incident. When Dwight Eisenhower declared that our U-2 plane was spying over the Soviet Union, it was the first time in the history of the world that a chief of state admitted his country was spying. I don't think Eisenhower knew Francis Gary Powers existed, or that the plane was even in the area. Perhaps his press secretary, James Hagerty, had forgotten to tell him.

I was a member of the Aeronautical and Space Sciences Committee at that time. We were shown photographs. We knew that the Russians knew that these flights were taking place. I think the only top official in Washington who *didn't* know was Eisenhower. However, Hagerty was so hurt over public criticism of the hours the President was spending on the golf course that he insisted Eisenhower "knew" all about the fact that the plane the Russians shot down was going on that day.

President Johnson and others have declared more than once that Eisenhower never knew what was going on. He certainly gave that impression. I think history will record he was a weak President who should be compared with another general who reached the White House, U. S. Grant.

After the changeover from the Eisenhower to the Kennedy administration there was an immediate and perceptible difference in the atmosphere of Washington. Youth and vitality were back in the town, there were new thoughts and ideas in the air. I remember thinking, "Now is the chance to get things done that we couldn't do under Eisenhower. Now this country will get moving again."

I must say I didn't expect John Kennedy to make quite as sturdy a President as he did. In an interview in November of 1960, just before his election, a young woman reporter quoted me as saying that I had seen him stripped in the gym and that I considered him too skinny. I never said anything like that. When we were both Representatives, I watched him play tennis and am certain he could have beaten me easily. As a matter of fact, at the Democratic convention I voted for him on that first ballot for Presidential nominee.

These conventions, by the way, strike me as tawdry exhibitions—grandstanding, clumsy clowning, drinking, stampeding and general hoopla. All mammoth political gatherings are abysmally undignified and awkward mechanisms for nominating candidates who will have the highest responsibilities.

Despite all my years in politics I had never attended one of these conventions until I was elected delegate-at-large for Ohio for the 1960 convention. There was far too much of the circus atmosphere at that brawl. I remembering having to silence a fellow delegate from Ohio during Senator Eugene McCarthy's inspiring nominating speech for Adali Stevenson. Kennedy won that nomination on his personality and energy. Adlai Stevenson is a wonderful man, an excellent Ambassador to the United Nations, but I think perhaps he is too smooth, too much the gentleman to capture completely the popular imagination. People seem to go for a politician who has the human failing of being at a loss for words sometimes.

One of the first things that seemed evident in Washington after President Kennedy's inauguration, was a feeling of horror among the Perle Mestas in the town; the elite were being driven out, the Jacobins were walking the streets. Some of the top political appointees of the Eisenhower administration immediately resigned and returned to private life.

A Washington taxi-cab driver once complained to me that highly placed Democrats in the Kennedy administration, new in Washington, were "tightfisted with their dough." He hoped they would be as close with "our millions" as they seemed to be with their own quarters. I hope he is pleased with Mr. Johnson.

Early in January I received my first invitation to the White House since my election. I remembered the receiving line of Roosevelt's day and noticed that there was none this time. The President and Mrs. Kennedy, Vice-President and Mrs. Johnson came down the stairway and mingled with the guests. I had known John F. Kennedy well as a fellow Congressman in the House of Representatives and when he was my colleague in the Senate. Both as Congressman and Senator he had been respected and well-liked. From his experience as a Representative and a Senator he was acquainted with practically every issue that came up for consideration. His successor has brought the same rich background to the job.

I have always admired Lyndon Johnson. When I came back to Washington after the Senatorial election in 1958 he was one of the first people I sought out. I had first known him during the early thirties when I was a Congressman-at-large and he was an ambitious young assistant to a Texas Congressman. Later, we served together in the House of

102

Representatives. I told him I wanted to be on the Aeronautical and Space Sciences Committee. He said, "Steve, anybody who can beat Bricker should have anything his heart desires." And he kept his promise.

Our founding fathers had envisioned the Senate as a body of older men, experienced men who would put a brake on the youthful impetuosity of the House of Representatives, by taking considered and conservative stands. It certainly hasn't worked that way in recent years. Senators have cleared the path for passage of the Federal Housing Act, for urban redevelopment, for federal aid to education, for a Youth Opportunities Act modeled on the old CCC of Franklin D. Roosevelt, for enlightened law-making of every kind that has often found itself blocked in the House of Representatives.

I think the first time I really knew we had entered a different era was not in Washington at all, but during a visit to Cleveland. I was having my dinner in a restaurant there when a waitress said to me, "You know, I just came back from Pennsylvania where I had a Kennedy dinner." I asked her what she meant. She explained that she had gone to visit her eighty-five-year-old mother and father in Madera, Pennsylvania, where they were living on a joint retirement income of fifty-five dollars a month. Before her visit her mother had written, "Don't bring food like you have always been doing during the past eight years. We are getting along fine now and will give you a Kennedy dinner." The waitress, whose name happens to be Doris Willard, said, "And that is just what happened. We had a wonderful meal—pork, potatoes au gratin, cheese, milk made out of powdered milk, even peanut butter cookies."

The Kennedy dinner to which Doris referred came about because one of the President's first orders was to increase the distribution of surplus foods with emphasis on meat and milk for the needy of this country, instead of the so-called "Mollygrub" handed out by the Eisenhower administration.

It was a privilege to serve under President Kennedy, even in the moments of severe tension when the world seemed on the verge of disaster, as at the time of the second Cuban crisis in October 1962. It seemed to me that under Eisenhower I was always having to vote *against* something— against crippling amendments that would hamstring labor unions, against the nomination of that whited sepulcher Lewis L. Strauss as Secretary of Commerce, against the President's veto of the 1959 housing act.

As a former President, Eisenhower once spoke against an Administration bill providing medical care for the elderly within social security. He used the scare words "socialized medicine." The bill proposing hospital and nursing home care for the elderly under social security coverage contained nothing whatever directing employment of physicians or interfering with the right of individuals to select their own doctors. This bill did not provide for, nor would it lead to, socialized medicine. In the same week following his speech, former President Eisenhower entered Walter Reed Hospital, an Army hospital, for treatment by government doctors. The fact is that from the time he was eighteen years old, he has consistently been a beneficiary of "socialized medicine." As a cadet at West Point, as an Army officer and as President, he was attended by government doctors, never by a private doctor, except when specialists were called in.

Under President Kennedy it was possible to vote for fair housing, fair labor standards, more social security for the aged, more federal assistance for schools and education, for the Peace Corps, for more unemployment compensation, for the urban redevelopment act, for Medicare, for trade expansion, for a national wilderness preservation system, for a national mental health program, for a transportation act.

However, the Senate debate on federal aid to education became quite violent at times. Everett Dirksen of Illinois, the Minority Leader, made an eloquent argument against

104

the federal school aid bill which the Senate eventually passed by an overwhelming vote. Hubert Humphrey of Minnesota made a strong speech for federal aid to construct schools and help pay teachers. Then the two continued their controversy in a running-fire debate. The debate was dramatic and most Senators agreed the Minority Leader was badly mauled. Senator Engle said, "I would as soon try to skin a wildcat in a phone booth as tangle with Hubert Humphrey on the Senate floor."

Most important, it was possible to vote for and to see passed a limited nuclear test ban treaty.

On May 1, 1960, following the U-2 incident and the clumsy handling of the affair by the Eisenhower administration, the prestige of this country was at its lowest point. In October 1962, when Kennedy confronted Khrushchev over the issue of Cuba, it rose to a tremendous height and it was never higher than upon the announcement that the Senate had passed the treaty to ban nuclear testing.

Shortsighted, narrow-minded, mean-souled persons again and again thwarted the intelligent programs of legislation outlined by Kennedy, but they will be forgotten when the programs are law and do honor to his name.

CHAPTER 8

⚑ *One of the things a man dreams of when he thinks about writing a book is the chance to sound off on all his pet gripes. I have a few. . . .*

As a Senator I have always found our government's cult of secrecy particularly infuriating. The fact is that pieces of paper are sometimes considered more valuable than human lives in official Washington.

Long before President Kennedy's tragic assassination, it had occurred to myself and others that there was no real security for any government representative in Washington. Anybody could walk into any Senator's office at any time and shoot him.

It is not so easy on the floor of the Senate. On the other hand, there was a man who *did* take a shot at Senator Bricker, right in the basement rotunda of the Senate Office Building as he was taking a subway car from his office to the Capitol. The would-be assassin was a real estate operator from Columbus. When Bricker had been Attorney General of Ohio, the man had lost some property—and blamed it on Bricker. Over the years he held his grudge and brooded over what had happened. (They tell me he lost all his property in the meantime, but that his derangement was also due, in part, to a brain tumor.) At any rate, he showed up one day in the Senate subway that leads from the Senate offices to the Capitol. As Senator Bricker was getting on the car, he came out of the rotunda and fired one shot. There is still a mark on the wall to commemorate the incident.

After a group of inflamed Puerto Ricans shot up several Congressmen from the gallery of the House and tried to assassinate President Truman, a precautionary measure was passed which requires anyone visiting the galleries of the Senate or the House of Representatives to get a pass first from the office of his Congressman or one of his Senators. But anyone can get a pass. They don't like you to carry anything in there, or point a finger or place things on the railings or wear hats, but it seems to me that these requirements are not enough to safeguard the elected representatives of the people.

However, just try to get a piece of paper out of the files!

They say because a stenographer made a mistake during the Cuba crisis in 1962, everything was in an uproar; the total machinery of government was jammed for an hour.

Recently, someone wanted to know how many people were in the CIA. He called the Soviet Embassy to find out.

In the room of the Senate Committee on Foreign Relations there is a locked cabinet. If any Senator wishes, as frequently happens, to get information on, say, the testimony of witnesses in closed or executive sessions of the committee, he must go to great lengths to get permission, and then they bring out a huge book which, as often as not, turns out to be full of tame items which have been published in every newspaper in the country. Yet one must go to the committee room since this material cannot be removed to a Senator's office.

Five days before the limited test ban treaty was initialed, I was called over to an executive session of the Armed Services Committee. Dean Rusk was a witness for three and a half hours. All this time there remained in front of me a copy of the test ban treaty text, which was short and simple, and the public was already aware of most of the details in it.

108

Yet, when the meeting broke up, the chief clerk checked us off with elaborate care as we handed back our copies.

I have tangled again and again with bureaucrats while trying to get simple information on matters related to pending legislation. I have more than once had the experience of locking up with furtive care in a special case some bit of information which had already leaked—if it had not, indeed, been deliberately released—to the nation's press.

One of the worst offenders is the State Department. More than once I have been through nonsensical rigmarole to obtain a few facts that were under their jurisdiction. There is supposed to be a liaison man in the department to accommodate Senators. You telephone him and leave a message. He never calls back.

Of course, it is essential that our top military secrets be kept out of the hands of potential enemies. But I think if this country placed more emphasis on the value of human lives and less on the sanctity of typewritten documents, we would all be better off.

Another thing that gets me down in Washington is Pentagonese gobbledygook. At the Pentagon, where hundreds of generals and admirals operate, flocks of new words and phrases fly out the doors. These are termed "Pentagonese" or "Washington Gobbledygook." I loathe it. These top officials presumably cannot consider using simple, readily understood language. For example, such and such a military depot is being *phased out;* it would not do to say *closed* or *abandoned.* If a decision has been delayed, it would seem simple to say so. But "delay" is a bad word—instead we have *a regression timewise.* Once I came across this phrase in Pentagonese: "Material resources of a surplus economy used to enhance its influence or protect its security in other parts of the world." *Program* refers to any assignment or task that cannot be completed by one phone call. Someone said the word *expedite* meant to confound confusion with commotion and that the word *channels,* or the phrase "this matter is going through channels," simply refers to the trail left by various interoffice memos written by one bureaucrat to another. There are *expediters* and *coordinators.* A coordinator is the fellow who has a desk between two expediters.

If a Senator telephones a department seeking information and is told, "we are making a survey and will report later," he knows that the bureaucrat hasn't done a thing but needs more time to think up an answer; and if the statement is made by a bureaucrat, "it's in process," then a Senator might as well conclude that the entire proposal is hopeless, being wrapped up in red tape. If the high-salaried department official says, "we'll look into it," that's final—unless the Senator inquires again, because by the time the wheel makes a full turn the bureaucrat assumes that the Senator will have forgotten about it, also.

Our foreign assistance officials prefer to use the term *vital sector.* Apparently, this means some country too proud to beg for money but not too humble to blackmail us by saying "you do this or we'll go to the Soviet Union." A *backward area* is an area really more backward than other backward areas. It is different, according to bureaucrats, from an underdeveloped area.

I guess we have all learned to live with the strange, graceless language employed in the communications of our armed forces, but when this sort of terminology begins to invade the halls of Congress, it makes me uneasy.

It went against the grain like chalk against a slate when Kenneth B. Keating, our distinguished Senator from New York, introduced a bill one day and coined one of the ugliest words I have ever heard, *urbiculture.* Senator Keating went so far as to propose that the President appoint a Secretary of Urbiculture. In Keating's own gobbledygook this would be a Cabinet officer to give consideration to the problems of city folk—a counterpart to our Secretary of Agriculture.

110

I have another word for Senator Keating—"agribusiness," or help for the family farmer!

When Alben Barkley was a Senator he once said, regarding verbal patterns in the U. S. Senate:

"If some colleague refers to you as 'the distinguished Senator from Ohio,' consider yourself lucky. If this same colleague refers to you as the 'able and distinguished Senator from Ohio,' be on your guard for the knife is getting sharper. If, however, your colleague refers to you as 'the able and distinguished Senator from Ohio and my good friend,' then duck fast because he's trying to see if the jugular vein is exposed. And, in case your colleague should refer to you as 'my very good friend, the able, distinguished and outstanding Senator from Ohio,' then run for your life!"

Verbal eccentricities are not the sole property of Congress, however. Representative Bill Moorhead of Pennsylvania is one of the topflight orators of the House. Immediately following a speech he made before the Daughters of the American Revolution, a young lady rushed up to him and said gushingly, "Oh, Congressman, your speech was superfluous! Simply superfluous!" "Thank you," replied Moorhead. "I'm thinking of having it printed posthumously." "Oh, that's wonderful," the lady said, "and the sooner the better!"

Another of my pet gripes as a Senator is the lack of discipline in the Senate Chamber. Visitors who have never been there always express surprise at the general rumble of noise and casual conversation that continues even when speeches are being made from the floor. I am particularly exasperated by administrative assistants who stand around idly at the sides of the room, posing for the gallery or insolently occupying the seats of members.

Then there is another brand of administrative assistant who likes to serve his country by lounging around the cafeteria offering oral reviews of everything that goes on in the

111

Senate and spending as little time as possible working at his desk.

I must say the men on my staff aren't like that. My administrative assistant, Herb Jolovitz, has proved himself an important, responsible public servant for the people of Ohio. He is discreet, intelligent, hard-working and quiet. He doesn't waste time. He isn't one of those porky rovers taking pay checks and returning little by way of service to the taxpayer. He was a lawyer in Canton, Ohio, but I hope it will be a long time before he returns to the practice of law.

Another of my pet peeves—although it is one which usually makes me more sleepy than angry—is the time-wasting speaker. Quite aside from the deliberate time-wasting by our filibustering neighbors from the South (I can't help thinking of them, sometimes, as on leave from another country—if not planet), there is another kind of Senator who simply cannot put anything briefly. The longest speech I myself ever gave was the one on civil rights. During the debate on Admiral Strauss's nomination, Senator Joe O'Mahoney's speech on the constitutional aspects of the right of the Senate to advise and consent to all nominations by the President will be remembered and cited long after Admiral Strauss has been forgotten. On the other hand, I came my nearest to dozing straight off during a preachment on the culture of the Far East offered to us by Senator Wallace F. Bennett of Utah.

The remarks of some Senators are better read than heard. John Williams of Delaware has a voice which lacks carrying power and his arguments are difficult to follow. Yet when you read his remarks in the *Congressional Record*, they are usually anything but boring.

Whenever a Senator reads in a monotonous tone a speech on a subject of interest solely to his home state, it is time to break out the toothpicks and prop up your eyelids. Allen Ellender of Louisiana, for instance, used to make me long for a quiet nap when I was a member of the Committee on Agriculture and Forestry. It was not uncommon for him to deliver a monologue which lasted from 10:30 in the morning to noon.

One day on the Senate floor hours were consumed debating a proposed national flower. Should it be a rose or a carnation? Senator Neuberger of Oregon, advocating the rose, said, "Unlike the corn tassel, the rose does not need price supports to make it flourish."

Senator Morton of Kentucky asserted, "Neither the rose nor the carnation, although beautiful, made any contribution to the welfare of our nation. On the other hand, the corn tassel is not a full flower. It is a male flower, the ear of the corn being female flower. I fear losing the women's vote if a male flower were adopted as the national flower emblem."

"Incidentally," he continued, "corn is converted into various products. Some of this conversion takes place in my native state of Kentucky and if the corn tassel is selected as the national flower, that might stir up the Anti-Saloon League."

Another matter which exasperates me is the technique of Congressional argument by which apples are compared with pears and the two equated. When we were trying to get through legislation to further the exploration of outer space by cooperation between Soviet and American astronauts, certain Senators suddenly started windy speeches about how the same money would be better spent on federal housing or education or feeding the hungry or clothing the weak or relieving the misery of the aged. But let a bill come up on low cost public housing or federal aid to education or Medicare, so-called, and these same fellows will vote it down. I say America is a rich country. We can afford to build decent housing and schools for our people, alleviate suffering, help encourage democratic nations in other parts of the world, and still get on with the exciting business of exploring the mysteries of the world and the universe around us.

On the other hand, I am against the wanton expenditure of money for foolish and futile enterprises. I am also opposed to king-sized salaries for federal officials. In 1963 I charged Representative Hays of my state with being too liberal in taking a home-town friend and a restaurant waiter on a tax-paid overseas junket. Congressman Hays retorted that *I* was being too liberal in accepting my salary of 22,500 dollars a year. He thinks legislators should be paid on a sliding scale from 5,000 to 35,000 dollars. I replied in turn that Representative Hays was a valuable but expensive member of Congress. His frequent overseas trips had earned him the nickname of Ohio's Marco Polo. I remember saying to Senator Talmadge of Georgia, "I understand Marco Polo was inclined to prevarication."

It is a good thing for men like Hays to travel and broaden their knowledge as legislators. But when Hays went to Rome a couple of years ago and saw the large shiny automobile waiting for him at the airport, he is reported to have given it a withering look and exclaimed, "Tell the Ambassador what he can do with this pile of tin!" The only limousine big enough to suit Hays in the entire city happened to be the Ambassador's, according to newspaper reports.

I believe public officials should be paid adequately. It would be unfortunate if only men and women of great wealth were able to occupy public office. I certainly don't advocate that. A Senator has tremendous expenses to pay out of his salary. He often has to maintain two homes—one in Washington and one in the state he represents. He is expected to entertain. He is expected to maintain a certain standard of living.

On the other hand, our government's only source of income for paying salaries is the taxpayer. In 1963, a committee headed by a retired Chicago steel executive made recommendations in its report to the President calling for really colossal salaries for officials in the legislative, judicial

114

and executive branches of our government. I think it would have been better if this committee had been made up of some university professors rather than retired steel executives and other wealthy men. Salaries should not be miserly. They should be comparable to those offered in private industry, up to a point. But when it is recommended that salaries of Supreme Court justices should be increased to 60,000 dollars a year, Cabinet officers to 50,000 dollars and that other officials get increases from 30,000 to 50,000 dollars a year, I think they have hit on a speedy way to empty the pockets of the taxpayer.

But why should administrators of independent agencies receive larger salaries than United States Senators? Senators seek election, often at great personal expense, maintain several residences, incur considerable travel and entertainment expenses. I make no complaint about this. It goes with the job. But Senators, contrary to a current popular impression, do not have expense accounts. Steel executives do.

After hearing my opinions and those of Senator Lausche on the subject of pay increases, Congressman Hays, pushing his amendment to pay legislators on a sliding scale, suggested that "each member decide for himself how much he is worth." He went on to say that "if my amendment passes and either of our Ohio Senators says he is worth more than 5,000 dollars, he should be tried for perjury." He was quick after this announcement to evaluate his own performance. "I am worth the maximum," he declared.

I remain in favor of realistic pay increases for all who work in the federal government. It may be necessary to raise the salaries of some in order to lure competent people into public service. I don't think it is necessary to legislate blanket raises for federal employees just for the sake of these few.

Another way to raise my blood pressure is to say the word "railroad." I don't feel sorry for this nation's railroads. I think the crises they are constantly experiencing are at least partially created by themselves. A couple of summers ago when I took the train from New York to Washington I found out at first hand why prospective railroad passengers stay away in droves. Four hours of traveling on a dirty, crowded, poorly-ventilated coach was convincing evidence that railroad officials regard passengers as necessary evils and make their real money carrying freight. There was no dining car or even a snack bar. Every coach was a candidate for the junk heap. (Maybe I took the wrong train.) That trip is the last one I intend to take from New York to Washington by train unless conditions change.

In contrast, it is a pleasure to ride in a country like Italy where the *Rapido* makes the long trip from Rome to Milan in six hours. The streamlined train is beautifully decorated and comfortable, yet the cost of the trip is less than air fare. One would think that under our free enterprise system railroad presidents would be way ahead of officials of government-operated Italian railroads. Perhaps railroad officials and unions should ask our government to invite Italy to send a reverse Peace Corps to the United States to teach our backward railroad operators how to take proper care of passengers, and at the same time earn money for dividends for their stockholders.

Another red flag for me is the visitor to our nation's capitol who dresses sloppily. Just about anything seems to go for some tourists during the blistering summer season. Outside the Senate Chamber and Reception Room, along the corridor to the Senate dining room and in the rotunda itself I have seen the most way-out garb—blue jeans, short shorts, tee shirts and slacks, too often on ladies of the light heavyweight class. I think it's wonderful that so many of our constituents come to the capitol in ever greater numbers, but I wonder how many of them would think of going to their own offices in shorts and a tee shirt.

All this time I have only been warming up to my really

116

pet, *pet* hate, which is the excesses of Washington social life. I don't deny that dinners or cocktail parties or receptions can be enjoyable, but it seems to me there is a limit. If I accepted every invitation I received, or even most of them, I could freeload every night of the week.

Frequently I am invited to banquets given by national organizations such as the Home Builders of America or the National Truckers Association, and letters come from Ohioans adding their personal wishes that I should accept. Nevertheless, when I arrive I frequently meet no one from my own state. Sometimes I briefly attend the reception preceding the dinner and then leave, particularly if I don't see a soul I know. At one of these affairs the speaker spoke insultingly of President Kennedy. I said, "I'm certainly paying too much for this meal if I am required to hear insults against my own party and our Chief Executive." I walked out.

And I am beginning to develop an allergy to the Washington reception. The freeloading that goes on is astounding. I have seen women bring along special paper bags and plastic containers and empty the hors d'oeuvres into them for later consumption. At one reception in an Arabian embassy two elderly ladies were gorging themselves at a huge table filled with shrimp cocktails and lavish quantities of sauce. During their feast a tall, dignified Arab gentleman in a white robe strolled by; one of the ladies actually wiped her hands on his robe.

If our parties are sometimes shockingly wasteful, what is to be said about the embassies of poverty-stricken countries whose representatives in Washington drive around in Cadillacs, rent magnificent embassy buildings and throw lavish parties while children in their own lands cry for a crust of bread? And what is their motivation? To impress our State Department officials, who are always among the most honored guests! Surely there must be something wrong with this method of maneuvering for aid.

117

Not all embassy visits turn out unpleasantly. In fact, I remember with no pain the time I went to the Soviet Embassy with several of my colleagues and their wives. It was shortly after Yuri Gagarin's trip. Going slowly up the steps Senator Gruening and I paused, being quite certain that all the guests would be photographed by the FBI. However, the gathering was friendly and informal. I talked with a young man attached to the embassy. We didn't discuss politics. He told me about his children and I told him about my grandchildren. A motion picture was the high point of the evening. I thought, "Here comes the propaganda." Instead, it was a beautiful love story of one day in the life of a Russian soldier in World War II.

At any rate, when I want to learn about a country overseas, the last place I would expect to find out anything much would be at a reception thrown by one of their embassies. Indeed, the only reliable way to find out about a country is to go there, and that is what I have done.

CHAPTER 9

🖎 *One of my admiring Ohio correspondents, seeking perhaps to outstrip me in brevity, once sent me the following mash note:*

"DEAR SENATOR:
  "Do me a favor. Get out of the country and stay there!"

I should like this anonymous supporter to know that I have taken his advice—at least part of it.

With jet travel, the world is constantly shrinking. It is feasible to visit every section of it without wasting time. As new countries emerge and the winds of freedom blow with ever-increasing force across Africa and the China Sea and, indeed, across the Western hemisphere, it is vital that those entrusted with our country's legislation see at first hand as many of these developments as they reasonably can.

Contrary to the popular impression that Senators travel free of charge, it has always turned out that these trips have cost me money, despite every courtesy that has been extended to me. On the other hand, I feel these personal expenditures were a splendid investment in terms of the knowledge I have been able to gain.

Actually, the most informative trip I ever took was my first excursion as a United States Senator in November of 1959. I took part in that "junket" at my own expense, not only as a Senator, but also as a reserve Army officer.

Eighteen made the journey, including Senator Cannon, Senator Moss, the chief clerk of the Senate Armed Forces Committee, and an Associated Press reporter—each one a reserve officer of the Air Force or the Army. We went to Hawaii, Wake Island, Okinawa, Manila, Hong Kong, Taiwan, Japan, Alaska and the Aleutian Islands, and Malmstrom Air Force Base in Montana, all in a period of about three weeks. Eighteen thousand miles of air travel—with briefings at Travis Air Force Base in California, Hickam Field in Hawaii, Clark Field near Manila, Okinawa and a meeting with Chiang Kai-shek and Madame Chiang—were climaxed, socially anyway, by a reception in Hong Kong at our consulate. Then on to Japan, where we did as much sightseeing as we could in the intervals between further Army and Air Force briefings and ambassadorial lunches.

Despite all we were shown, I remain firm in the opinion that a Senator who has spent three weeks in the Far East should not feel he is ready to form definite conclusions as to American foreign policy in that part of the world. I did come home, though, with the impression that Red China is potentially a far more dangerous enemy to the United States than the Soviet Union has been or will be. On the other hand, it seemed to me that there was little likelihood of another Pearl Harbor. God willing I am never proved wrong!

During December and January of 1960-61 I spent a few weeks in England, Germany and Italy as a member of the Senate Aeronautical and Space Sciences Committee, with a brief stopover in Switzerland. While we were in England, I was fascinated by Jodrell Bank, where the great radio telescope probes the universe and where many defense installations are located. In England, also, I had the pleasure of interviewing the Right Honorable Viscount Hailsham, Lord Privy Seal and professor of science, and Professor H. W. Massey of the physics department at University College. In

Bonn I met Germany's Minister of Defense, Franz Joseph Strauss, who had served as a major in the German Army on the Eastern front, and in Aachen discussed defense matters with Professor A. W. Quick; in Rome, I saw Professor Francesco Jordoni, professor of the national research committee of Italy, and Professor Luigi Broglio, head of an aeronautical engineering school. The Italian newspapers, I was happy to see, favored in their headlines quotations of my hopes for the closest cooperation between the United States and Italy in space research.

When I left Rome, to sustain me through memories of English food while flying over London, I read with great absorption a two-page menu from Maxim's in Paris, which I had picked up in transit.

In July 1960, I left the Democratic National Convention in Los Angeles—even though Senator Kennedy had invited me to join him on the platform when he was to deliver his acceptance speech—in order to keep a rendezvous at the United States military cemetery in Carthage, Tunisia, as a member of the commission appointed by Vice-President Nixon to dedicate some of our military cemeteries abroad.

En route to North Africa I spent two days in Paris where I attended dedication ceremonies at St. Devold. At a noonday banquet which preceded the St. Devold dedication I found myself suddenly in an argument with Mrs. Amory Houghton, the wife of our Ambassador to France at the time. She had been bitterly denouncing Senator John F. Kennedy all during the first course. She complained that Senator Kennedy, in his address accepting the nomination from the Democratic party, had declared that President Eisenhower had commenced the Republican campaign in 1952 by making a trip to Korea and now he was ending his administration in 1960 by not going to Japan.

"But that statement is factually correct," I told Mrs.

Houghton. What the United States needed was a strong President, I added, instead of a weak one, and I believed and hoped that President would be John Kennedy. I felt a distinct draft from Mrs. Houghton's side of the table for the rest of the meal.

Later during the luncheon I happened to mention this incident to our Ambassador to Great Britain. He said he supposed it was all right to have undiplomatic diplomats, but it was rather alarming to have an undiplomatic wife of an ambassador.

Having been in North Africa during the war, going there again brought back to mind all the squalor and ugliness of warfare. The mosquitoes of North Africa had not forgotten me. They found me in my room at the Hotel Majestic in Tunis and welcomed me like an old friend. They even followed me into the lobby.

I made a speech at the cemetery which was not quite as short as the Gettysburg Address—mine lasted eleven minutes—but I tried to keep it as simple as I could. I expressed the hope that hundreds of years from now the Americans who had lost their lives in World War II and who are buried in that cemetery will be spoken of reverently at a time when the world is free from threats of dictatorship and aggression and when men and women the world over have been restored to their simple dignity as creatures of God.

With me during the ceremonies, among those members of the committee from the United States, were Mrs. Wendell L. Willkie, Admiral Thomas C. Kinkaid, and Generals Benjamin Davis, Jacob Devers and Thomas North.

Afterwards, I went through the entire cemetery, noting especially the names and locations of the crosses for Ohio soldiers. Later, I wrote to the next-of-kin whenever it was possible to obtain their addresses.

I went for a stroll through the ruins of Carthage, saw part of a Roman bath from the fifth century and the traces of

122

Punic architecture left by the Romans after the final Punic War, when they destroyed the city and killed its inhabitants, plowed the ground and sowed it with salt so that nothing could grow. But the Americans buried in the cemetery at Carthage had lived through days and nights when it seemed that the last vestiges of sanity, decency and kindness had disappeared from the face of the earth. They had witnessed the creation of man-made ruins far worse than ancient Carthage.

In December 1960, Senator Dennis Chavez and I flew to Central America—first to Mexico, then to Guatemala, where Robert F. Corrigan, a fellow Clevelander who was counselor of the embassy and deputy chief of the mission, met us and brought us to his home. The President of Guatemala later took us on a long air trip over the Guatemalan mountains. I noticed that he was in uniform and armed with an automatic. The pilot had a .45 caliber automatic also—with the safety-catch off. As a matter of fact, the president had recently supervised, from this same little plane, the bombing of Puerto Barrios Air Strip while suppressing a revolt to drive him from office. Since then he has gone the way of many Latin American dictators and is in exile due to a revolt that succeeded.

In the Guatemalan countryside we saw the straw-thatched huts where the Indians live much as they always have, except for the fact that many have turned to Catholicism. There are Mormon and Protestant as well as Catholic missionaries in Guatemala, but the Catholics have been the most successful, judging from the large number of crosses in evidence at Indian villages.

It seems to me that with all the money we are spending in Guatemala and in other Latin American countries it ought to be possible to make the water in these countries drinkable

123

and to provide power plants and dams so that they may build up their own private industries. I also believe that these countries should build secondary highways connecting with the main Inter-American Highway. In Guatemala, for example, I was shocked to learn that many thousands of pounds of bananas had to be thrown away because they couldn't be transported from the hinterlands to Puerto Barrios for export.

In Costa Rica the chargé d'affaires of the embassy, Roy Irwin Kimmell, confided in me that he intended to return to Rhode Island and run for Congress. This seemed to me optimistic, in view of the fact that he had been away in the diplomatic service for many years.

Nicaragua, which followed Honduras on our itinerary, had recently had quite a bit of its territory handed over to Honduras by the World Court. I was relieved that the president and his brother, who was commander of the armed forces, did not ask us to get it back for them. We traveled along the 150-mile Rama Road, an east-west highway representing a partially-fulfilled commitment made by Franklin Roosevelt. Nicaragua in 1942 had passed in its congress a bill leasing a strip of land to the United States for a canal. Later we decided we didn't want a Nicaraguan canal and, when the Nicaraguans protested, we agreed to pay for a direct road between the cities of San Benito and Rama. Our taxpayers shelled out nearly thirty million dollars for the Rama Road.

In Panama, as in many other countries I have visited, I noticed that Americans living there tended to isolate themselves from the people of the country. This clannishness, together with the colonialist attitude which seems to have been picked up where the British left off, as it were, is extremely important whenever anti-American feeling reaches a boiling point. The acts of hostility against us are blamed on Communist infiltration, but it is usually ourselves, by our lack of true democratic interest in the lives of the average citizens

124

in these lands, who sow seeds for resentment which enemy propagandists find it all too easy to exploit.

In May of that year, Senators Cannon, Moss and myself were once more traveling together, this time to Paris, mainly to represent our country at an international air show, and in July of the same year I flew to the Scandinavian countries, along with other members of the Senate Committee on Public Works. In Oslo, the Prime Minister of Norway and other officials discussed the European situation with us in great detail. All of them agreed that Americans overrated the power of the Soviet Union.

We went into the interior of Norway, sleeping overnight during the trip on sheets stuffed with feathers. We inspected power installations and saw one which was completely underground, eliminating the need for painting and many repairs. Some of these underground installations dated from the time of the German occupation during World War II. In Sweden we inspected many hydro-electric projects.

There is, of course, much to see in Norway and Sweden besides power plants, but it was helpful to the work of our committee to get a first-hand look at what these middle-of-the-road countries have been able to achieve through intelligent use of water power, turning to peaceful uses installations originally intended for purposes of warfare.

In September I traveled to England, Switzerland, Italy, France and Portugal. I learned that in England, which would certainly bear the brunt of any attack from an enemy, the officials were not even giving instructions on first aid methods. In the past, the Home Secretary handled civil defense matters. I didn't see any frantic rush to build air raid shelters.

My encounters with English officers during my wartime experiences in Italy had been rather unpleasant, and this had tended to color my feelings in general about their country. Whenever I am in England I always sort of wish I were in some other country. Yet there is something so vital and invigorating about the atmosphere of London that even a prejudiced fellow like myself cannot help feel his step quicken when he reaches that city. London is a man's town.

My visit this time was mainly in connection with the formal opening of the Commonwealth Parliament session in the Houses of Parliament. I must admit that for pomp and display the English beat all the world. Later, there was a reception at Lancaster House where I felt that I was part of a captive audience. It was three hours before the Queen and her husband chose to leave. It seemed to me that the Duke of Edinburgh, who looked bored while the Queen was addressing Parliament, was acting in a way strangely familiar to me, and then I realized what it was: he was performing at that reception like a candidate for the legislature or the city council seeking votes. He paid particular attention to delegates from newly-formed nations in Africa. He shook hands with me, but we didn't have much to say to each other.

I attended sessions of the conference every day for a week. When I wasn't listening to the debates, I held conversations with government officials. The answer of one of them to a question of mine was typical.

"Do you think there will be war between the Soviet Union and the United States?" I asked. His reply: "Not unless you Yanks by your aggressive acts bring it on."

One evening I was interviewed on BBC-TV. The next day, among many other telephone calls, I got one from some man at the station who said he was sending me a contract for my signature since the station intended to send me a check! I had to make one change in the BBC contract: they called the Union Commerce Bank of Cleveland the "Bank of Cleve-don."

From England we proceeded to Copenhagen, Düsseldorf, Geneva and then on to Bern. In Copenhagen I found the same attitude toward air raid shelters as in England, but in Bern the attitude was just the opposite; many homes had air raid shelters. The Swiss government was requiring apartment dwellers and home owners to build shelters at their own expense; there is no income tax deduction allowable for this purpose.

Scarcely more than a month later I was on my way to South America. This turned out to be the most enlightening of all the tours I have taken as a Senator.

Senators McGee, Moss and Engle joined with me later in writing an extensive report on that month-long journey which took us to Venezuela, Peru, Bolivia, Chile, Argentina, Paraguay, Brazil and British Guiana. During twenty-six days we traveled more than 20,000 miles by air, nearly 1,000 by auto and ship, and thousands of miles by boat on the Amazon and the Rio Negro Rivers in Brazil.

Our target areas ranged from steamy jungles to dry plateaus. In some places we were among the first official visitors from the United States. Our intent was to gauge the conditions in South America for the President's new Alliance for Progress program, especially the attitudes of the people in the various countries We were interested not only in what officials thought, but in what the man in the street thought. This was an ambitious program for a one-month trip, yet we learned a great deal.

Wherever we went we were treated courteously. There were no anti-American demonstrations. Our conclusions were that the Alliance for Progress seemed the most exciting new idea in South America, but there was deep urgency felt that speed would be critical and that short-range, quick-impact projects would be essential for psychological reasons in South America. We also came to some other conclusions: that cold war machinations were increasing, that Castroism and anti-Americanism ran far more deeply than was consoling for us to admit, and that to deal realistically and helpfully in its relations with South America the United States would have to take all these factors into account.

I remember looking down from our luxurious hotel in Caracas at the *favellas* on the hillside, the squalid shacks, and later seeing still more of the misery and hunger afflicting Venezuela's people—sores on the legs of the children suffering from malnutrition, distended stomachs—all this not far from our hotel with its beautiful swimming pool, with the orchestra playing in its garden restaurant; all this close to apartment buildings where rentals go upward from $250 a month; all this in a country rich in resources, where tyranny, failure to tax equitably, distribute land and provide sanitation have plunged 95 percent of the people into poverty.

We talked with President Betancourt, we met his cabinet officers and members of their families. The President's hand had been crippled and burned in an assassination attempt on him some months before. He asserted that Castro was behind the attempt. He spoke of the shortage of teachers, of unemployment, of inflation. Since that time his term of office has expired, and he is one of the minority of Latin American presidents who served out their elected terms.

In Lima, Peru, I saw slums worse than those in any Hooverville in the United States during the depression. I saw children and men and women looking for food in scrap piles. Later in Cuzco, the ancient capital of the Incas, we saw naked, hungry youngsters, old before their time.

Senator Engle and I took long walks in Lima without supervision. Getting away from officials who want to direct you and censor what you see was the wonderful thing about the South American trip—the opportunity to visit the people of the country and see for ourselves, do at least a little investigating on our own.

In Bolivia, I was impressed by our Ambassador, Ben Stephansky. He seemed to me our outstanding ambassador on that continent. Once again, in that coffee-and-tin rich country, we saw old-looking faces on solemn children at La Paz, despite the fact that a large part of all American aid to South American republics has gone to Bolivia. But in Bolivia it was asserted that officials in our embassies had urged land reform. Of course, the land owners opposed any income taxes against *them,* or any attempt to persuade them to divest themselves voluntarily of any of their holdings for government distribution.

At the Hotel Carrera in Santiago, Chile, a United States Trade Mission had reserved a small section of the main lobby for an evening exhibit, decorating the wall with a huge American flag and President Kennedy's picture. Eleven strapping young Russians—members of a Soviet soccer team —sprawled on the best chairs directly beneath the Stars and Stripes and the President's portrait. Invited guests and members of the American Trade Mission began to arrive for the scheduled proceedings. Some of them, along with hotel officials, tried to talk in English, Russian, Spanish and German with the Soviet team leader, pointing out chairs in other parts of the large lobby. Not a Russian moved. At first a young lady, an American tourist, was merely interested as a spectator. Finally, she walked over to stand before the chairs occupied by the Russians, pointed to the team leader and the Stars and Stripes prominently displayed in the background, and aimed her camera. In an instant the Soviet soccer team members looked horrified and leaped out of range. The trade mission moved in. The girl tourist laughed and said, "See, no film, but did those characters scram!" Later, our Ambassador tried in vain to locate and thank this quick-thinking American; and Chileans are still talking about the incident.

We spent most of our time in Chile looking at the ambitious agricultural projects of the country. The United States has been extending technical assistance to Chile since 1943, with agricultural development as the principal goal. Our two governments have also cooperated for a long time in cultural and scientific fields.

Chile in the fifties underwent a series of natural disasters, including terrible earthquakes. Our government responded promptly to calls for help with one of the largest emergency relief operations ever undertaken under the Mutual Security Program.

The country is vast with huge deserts, the skyscraping Andes, a resort area of lakes and, further south, the always cold area of Tierra del Fuego. Most of the people of Chile (30 percent are white, 5 percent Indian and the rest *mestizo—* of mixed race) live in the long, luxuriant valley in the center of the country. Our agricultural experiments, in cooperation with Chile's, have taken place mostly in this area. With so little time at our disposal, it would not be fair for me to say that I came away with anything more than an impression of a country trying earnestly to make the most of its resources for the sake of its people.

In Argentina we suddenly found ourselves taking care of seven freeloaders imposed upon us by our Buenos Aires embassy. They either wanted to view our activities and report back to some CIA official or to the Ambassador, or they figured they would spend a relaxing few days with a Senatorial party, I don't know which. This irritated me quite a bit. I was also chagrined by the fact that, although we had specifically requested "No entertainment," nevertheless, without any prior consultation, we were taken to a restaurant where a huge gaucho party in our honor went on for hours. Then the chairman of our committee was presented with the check, not only for ourselves, but for some sixty other guests. We paid for our Senatorial party only.

After Argentina came Paraguay, and then again in Brazil poverty cried out—poverty that was not a blight of nature but the curse of oppression and mismanagement. The sugar plantations of Brazil and the interior country are far more fertile than any land in Ohio, but the per capita income in northeastern Brazil, in Recife and vicinity, is far under one hundred dollars a year. Ninety-five out of a hundred people in Recife live in squalor and go hungry to their beds. Yet many of the smug officials in our embassies, who would not think of visiting a Brazilian or sharing ten minutes with him if it could possibly be avoided, denounce as Communists South Americans who advocate land reform.

However, in Brazil we had quite an adventure when a pilot bringing Senator Engle and myself down an alligator-infested tributary of the Amazon stalled his craft. I had warned him that the stream looked too shallow, but he said it was the best way to get to a lake we wanted to see. When his craft lurched to a stop after the engine conked out, I found myself staring in horrified fascination at the alligators sliding into the water while the afternoon light faded. Clair Engle himself, who turned out to have an unsuspected knowledge of boat engines, got it going again. The mosquito bites we received while waiting for him to fix the engine lasted a long time.

In all these countries—and the same goes for British Guiana, and those parts of the British West Indies which we were able to visit—it seemed to me that many of the difficulties in our relations, just as in Central America, came from the fact that we sent ambassadors who lived in ivory towers, instead of men toughened through experience and willing to rub shoulders with the people of the land where they represented us. I made personal reports about three officials, suggesting their dismissal or transfer. One American

131

consul in Brazil even appeared to boast of the fact that he had never been in the homes of any Brazilian nationals nor invited any Brazilians to his home.

Everywhere sanitation, education, land reform, slum clearance were the obvious antidotes for the ills which have kept the masses in hunger and ignorance. Yet in too many of these countries I found right-wing consuls and narrow-minded officials who seemed to think that we could go on with impunity forever, ignoring the needs of the millions in South America without paying the price of losing our allies to totalitarian rule. I got the feeling that South America had become a sort of Siberia for our State Department officials. I also began to wonder whether we hadn't sent too much money and aid overseas to Europe and the Far East and too little to the continent to the south of us.

The end result of our foreign aid to South America is to make the rich richer and the poor poorer, to entrench more firmly the corrupt overlords so that the bulk of the people are obviously more likely to resent than be grateful to a provider at once so generous and so unjust. From our own viewpoint, on the other hand, it would be tragic if these unhappy aspects were to curtail our foreign aid program—now more vital than ever before. In fact, we can no more bring an end to our foreign aid program than can the richest man in the United States refuse to contribute to his town's Community Chest.

In March 1962, I made a brief visit to Hawaii as chairman of a Public Works subcommittee to inspect that new state, and in November of the same year I once again returned to Europe, spending time in Paris, West Berlin, Frankfurt, Vienna, Munich, Rome and Madrid, an extremely worthwhile and instructive trip.

In spite of all I had read about West Berlin, I found it

startling to see, in 1962, the astonishing prosperity and booming industry of that Western showcase. Although it seems childish to maintain old hostilities endlessly, when one is in Germany one cannot help being haunted by the familiar but unanswerable question: "Who won the war, anyway?"

I made a tour of the Berlin Wall, a wall of shame that stands as a stark expression of Communist defeat in this world, a symbol that Communist leaders fear peaceful co-existence. Here is a demonstration in barbed wire and bleak mortar for all to see that Communists the world over are able to hold sway over their captive peoples only by force of arms, by terroristic methods and by isolation.

In February 1963, Senator James B. Pearson of Kansas and I were appointed by Vice-President Johnson to the United Nations conference in Geneva on the "application of science and technology."

It is my private opinion that the science conference at Geneva was a State Department boondoggle, an example of futility and waste, with American taxpayers footing 40 percent of the cost. I was willing enough to take time out from my Washington duties to attend, and I swallowed without comment my economy class seat on the plane arranged by State Department officials, though I must say that my first trip to Europe by convoy twenty years before was more comfortable.

At the conference, speaker after speaker addressed the delegates. I lost count after the first twenty-one. I watched the delegates from developing nations, and became increasingly confident that they couldn't possibly grasp much of what was said, or care. I became acquainted with a young man from Nigeria who was having a terrible time trying to follow the highly technical statements; he finally gave up.

Our State Department should have seen to it that our

133

AID and foreign service personnel already abroad provided the necessary groundwork for delegates to an extremely technical conference of this kind. Our neighbors from Canada sensibly showed motion pictures which graphically illustrated the information they wanted to convey. Despite my voluble expression of these opinions at the time, the handout from the State Department quoted me as saying: "Senator Stephen M. Young of Ohio proposed that the United States employ roving teams of technical and information experts to help developing nations make the most of challenging large scale international conferences."

I made no such suggestion. I do not want additional bureaucrats feeding at the public trough.

I felt that Senator Pearson, who is serious-minded and able, and I wasted our time at the Geneva conference; it seemed to me that the many experts and scientists were also wasting theirs.

Travel has taught me as much about some of my colleagues as about the countries I have visited. There are some, whose names I do not wish to mention, who will not be my traveling companions again if I can help it. On a study mission to another land, with time at a premium, I don't like to have my days wasted by uncooperative men whose only interest is in socializing, who think more about picking up bargains and gifts than learning about the lands they are visiting and making contact with the people who live there.

I don't like men who ask foolish, time-consuming questions at briefing sessions.

I don't like irresponsible travelers who are late and hold up planes.

I do think the most valuable time I have spent abroad has been in visiting undeveloped areas rather than big, familiar cities like Paris and London and Rome. I also believe Senators would learn more if they were allowed to do more exploring on their own. An intelligent escort officer can be of great value and save you a lot of time. But it is not helpful for a traveler to be too sheltered and directed. He ought to get around and see places and people for himself.

AID—the Agency for International Development—is our foreign assistance program. I am glad we are calling it "foreign assistance" these days and not using the subterfuge title "mutual security." I think the greatest sickness that infects our aid programs is the relaxed Americans who live high on the hog overseas as employees of this and other agencies and who do little work of importance for our country. I object to their palatial homes, their government-supplied air conditioners, their cut-rate food and liquor. As one constituent wrote me, "The ostentatious way of living by our government employees does not go down well in lands where peoples have about twenty cents a day to live on." That is one reason I am in favor of the Peace Corps—overseas help that brings trained young people into significant relationships with the citizens of the countries they visit.

Sometimes I think that at least half the money we have spent on these countries has been wasted. It has not gone to the people who need it but has found its way into the pockets of corrupt and unscrupulous men. And I think I have learned something else; money can buy recovery for a tottering economy, yes. This was certainly demonstrated in the postwar years in countries like France and Italy. But money can never buy loyalty or friendship, anywhere. Dollars alone can never buy genuine friendship—among nations any more than between individuals.

I didn't join the Senate to see the world, but I am certainly glad I have had the chance to see so much of it. It has helped me in my work, and I hope the Ohio correspondent mentioned at the beginning of this chapter is as happy about that as I am.

135

CHAPTER 10

🖎 *In the summer of 1958, when I was campaigning for the United States Senate, I heard a scornful voice shout from the rear of the hall where I was speaking: "I've read you are sixty-eight years old. The Senate has enough old men already!" "Listen, Buster," I hollered back, "I feel like I'm forty!"*

I don't think age today is the handicap it once was. People say I look youthful. One fellow said, "You look your name." Well, I feel that way.

My hair may be gray, but my skin is not. I am five feet eight inches tall and I try to keep my weight down to 154 pounds. I don't think my physical fitness is an accident. There is rarely a day when I don't get down to the Senate gym. There I let masseurs pummel me, I pull weights, I swim. I like tennis and I play it often. As a Senator, I work harder than I did during my many years as a trial lawyer.

I think the concept that people should quit working at sixty-five is completely absurd. Sixty-five may have been old for most men eighty years ago. It isn't now. I would like to see compulsory retirement scrapped. Retirement at sixty-five should be voluntary only. At the same time, I think the present limit of 1,200 dollars a year on outside earnings for anyone living on social security should be doubled or tripled.

Ours is a youth-oriented nation, but there are in America

seventeen million men and women who have reached their sixty-fifth birthday. In another twenty years there will be twenty million. Most of them don't have an adequate income or a private pension or health and hospitalization insurance. Yet more than eleven million of these people will live to be seventy-five, nearly five million to be eighty-five.

What good is the honorary title Senior Citizen to them if they have to live as second-class citizens? Anyway, I'm allergic to that cognomen, Senior Citizen.

Scores of Senators and Representatives in our present Congress have passed the age of sixty-five. More than thirty of us are over seventy-five. At seventy-five Eleanor Roosevelt was still making important contributions to our nation and to the world. Her schedule would have exhausted most teenagers.

Just because Bismarck, back in Germany in the 1870's, established sixty-five as the eligible age for government benefits when the first social security plan was instituted, here we are—stuck with arbitrary cutoff.

In 1935, as a member of the House of Representatives, I voted for the first social security law. In 1949, as a member of the House Ways and Means Committee, I helped draft an amended version of that law. When I think that the average person on social security gets 68 dollars a month from the government—816 dollars a year—*if* he earns no more than 1,200 dollars from outside sources, I am deeply troubled.

I will never forget that in the fall of 1961 Congress saw fit to provide medical care for hogs—to cure hog cholera—but not for needy men and women under social security.

Anyhow, I think the cliché that "you can't teach an old dog new tricks" cannot be applied to human beings. Scientific experiments on learning ability have demonstrated that the more motivation there is, the better the student is able to learn. In other words, mental powers don't decline when middle age is over.

138

Senator Theodore Green of Rhode Island only recently, at ninety-two, announced his voluntary retirement from the Senate. (He is still active as chairman of the board of a bank in his state.) He managed to retain his sense of humor even after a lifetime of political activity. Once he got into a Washington taxi-cab with a friend. When they reached their destination, he paid the driver. As the cab pulled away, the Senator said, "Well, there's one vote I can count on." "Why?" asked the friend. "Did you give him a big tip and tell him to vote Democratic?" "No, indeed," said Senator Green. "I didn't tip him at all and told him to vote Republican."

Next to the question about my age, I am asked most often, "Senator, how did you become a liberal?" People point to my small-town, strait-laced background. They remind me that I didn't grow up in the slums, never went hungry and yet have always been on the side of the underdog, voted with liberals, fought for the rights of the have-nots. I like to point out that there have been other liberals far better off than I ever was. Franklin Roosevelt didn't grow up in a log cabin and neither did John F. Kennedy. I suppose you would call my own upbringing middle class. It is certainly a term I am not ashamed of.

I was born in a place called Puckerbrush Township. If you follow the map of Ohio carefully enough and don't drive too fast, eventually you will find yourself there, close by Norwalk, the county seat of Huron, Ohio. What was formerly Puckerbrush Township is a part of East Norwalk and the town has grown until it sprawls eastwards toward Wakeman and Oberlin.

Yet the Puckerbrush Township of sixty years ago is still recognizable today. Farm country still rolls out from Norwalk, the air is as pure as it ever was, unpolluted by factory smoke, and the scar of the stone quarry remains—the only identifying mark for the casual observer to distinguish this neighborhood from hundreds of others like it over the Ohio landscape.

A climate of certainty and optimism, of placid conviction that progress is a train whose wheels will click steadily on until it reaches the last stop at the hypothetical dream city of Utopia, U. S. A., still pervades Puckerbrush Township now as it did in the last decade of the nineteenth century. The place is like a child enjoying a relaxed snooze, safe in its mother's lap.

I was the fourth of five children, but I could never claim I was neglected because the family was large. We never went hungry and we never endured any of the hardships that were commonplace among Americans in the days of the great depression nearly half a century later, when I began my career as a Congressman. There was, of course, another side of the railroad tracks, and rumors of difficulties among the deprived, usually traceable, it was felt, to their own lack of spunk and enterprise.

A little charity could always oil the wheels, and the train would roll on, ever closer to the day when all America would be one big, comfortable middle class. My boyhood hero was Horatio Alger, but if I were to rise to riches it could never be from rags. The Youngs were not rich, but we were never poor, either. Each year, little by little, we climbed the modest rungs of economic betterment, able to afford a bit more ease—perhaps never too much, certainly never too little. I grew up assuming that was the way it went for just about everybody in the world.

Though we weren't poor, my mother liked to economize. She used to go on budget-reducing drives, which must have braced me for similar experiences as a government employee later on. For instance, she would decide that food expenditures were too high. Then for a couple of days that week we children could expect mush and milk for supper. My younger sister, Belle—her nickname was Babe for reasons lost in the mists of antiquity as was my nickname of Pet—didn't appreciate mush and milk suppers much, and neither did I. It was during one of them that my mother scolded me, "Pet, never talk with mush in in your mouth."

Stephen M. and Belle W. (Wagner) Young were as respectable a pair of parents as you're liable to run across in a yellowing tintype. Mother was always a bit on the thin side, but there was a gentleness in her nature usually associated with the plumper mother-image of her day. At the same time, she had strict ideas about Sunday school attendance for us children and the consumption of alcohol, as well as the rights of parents, which were always inviolate in that era. My father exuded confidence, character and solidity from every inch of his substantial frame. There's a photograph of him over my desk in the Old Senate Office Building, wearing a Masonic key and looking as stern as a deacon. He wasn't though, really. Later I used to wonder why we lived on a farm at all in those early days, not only because my father was a lawyer and had to commute to his office in the nearby city of Norwalk every day, but because he was one of the most gregarious men I ever knew. It's still hard for me to imagine him surrounded by fields and trees instead of by hearty and well-fed companions.

Life was not lonely or austere for the Youngs, with five offspring to make a six-room house seem smaller than it probably was. Three of the children were older than I; my sister Walburga, called Wally, was ten years ahead of me. My brothers Henry and Don John were older, too. The only one I could really lord it over was my sister Belle; I beat her by a year and a half. Belle and I are the only ones left now, but while the others lived we were a close-knit family. Wally, in particular, was close to me. She helped raise me, in fact, and was always sure of my future.

Considering my reputation for a tart tongue and a warm

temper, I apparently got along well with my brothers and sisters. Not that we didn't enjoy our full quota of sibling rivalry, even though they didn't have a scientific name for it at the time. For example, one day I was having a good old-fashioned row with my bigger brother Don—which reached such proportions that I started to chase him around with a hatchet. My mother shouted, "Pet, you come right inside this instant!" "Wait until I kill Don," was my succinct reply. (I have been replying succinctly ever since.) We were a lively clan.

Before I was five we moved away to the town of Norwalk itself, where my father had his law office. Norwalk is in what is known as the Western Reserve Firelands, and was named after Norwalk, Connecticut. During the Revolutionary War the English Navy burned some towns in Connecticut, including Norwalk. After the Revolution, Congress awarded two counties in Ohio to the Connecticut people whose homes had been burned. They were also given land in the area by Congress as a kind of veterans' bonus. That is why they call the area the Firelands and why it was settled by former Connecticut dwellers. You might say the settlers of Norwalk, Ohio, were displaced persons of the Revolutionary War.

When we moved to Norwalk it was a few years before the turn of the century and there were about 7,000 people living there. I guess nearly every one of them knew my father. He had started out in life as a Republican, but had switched to the Democratic party during the William Jennings Bryan campaign in 1896 and stayed a Democrat until the day he died in 1922. His own father found it almost impossible to forgive him for abandoning the Republican side, but everyone in Norwalk went on loving him.

My father was a trial lawyer in general practice. As a lawyer he was wonderful, but as a businessman rather less so. He used to say, "A lawyer works hard, lives well and dies poor." Later he became a Common Pleas judge of Huron

142

County—in other words, the judge of a trial court of unlimited jurisdiction.

My mother wasn't interested in politics, but she shared one passion with her husband—an absolute and uncompromising hatred of social injustice. They were both tolerant, fairly easy-going people, but lies and cruelty and injustice made their blood boil.

I used sometimes to visit my father's law office on the second floor of a building across from the county courthouse and I remember how awed I was by the bulk of his big, low desk, made of some invincible wood like oak, and cluttered with mysterious, solemn-looking papers. I knew from the first time I went there that I wanted to be a lawyer. I grew up believing, like the Lord Chancellor in Gilbert and Sullivan's "Iolanthe," that:

"The law is the true embodiment
Of everything that's excellent."

Yet I was still a small boy when an incident occurred in Huron, a nearby town, which shook my faith in the absolute rightness of those who enforce the law. The town marshal had arrested an emaciated, poorly dressed man. Another boy and I saw him strike the man, who wasn't resisting arrest. We followed them down to the jail, and all the time the marshal was beating up his prisoner, who kept begging over and over just to be let alone. The man wasn't hitting back, he was simply pleading for mercy. Blood was trickling out of his mouth.

I shouted, "Someone ought to stop that." The marshal turned around, fixing mean eyes on my friend and me. "You kids say something and you'll get worse," he warned us, brandishing his club.

Since then I have witnessed infinitely more wanton cruelty—especially in Europe during and after World War II—but I never forgot the marshal and his club. Now I knew what my father and mother meant about injustice, and why

143

they hated it, and I have never stopped hating it since then, or ever hesitated to speak up to protest it.

Neither my mother nor my father had too much time to indulge me with the rest of the family to think about, and it was really my older sister, Wally, who did most to help bring me up. She got that name, Walburga, by the way, after my mother's mother, who also had good reason to hate injustice, having married a revolutionary against the King of Prussia in the middle of the nineteenth century. The Revolution of 1848, in which her husband was involved against the Crown in Germany, was put down and my grandparents, with many other Germans, emigrated to the American Midwest.

When I was about six my father took me to a meeting of the Democratic party in Milan, Ohio. It was my first political meeting and I was strongly impressed by my father's oratory. When he made some reference to "the noblest Roman of them all" I thought it was his own phrase. I was overwhelmed with pride. When I was about ten I was in the audience to hear a speech he gave at the Jackson Day Banquet —a traditional annual dinner of the Democratic party. In that speech he said something I never forgot:

"There are just two theories of government. One is to legislate for the rich and well-to-do, hoping that some of the prosperity will trickle down to those below. The other is to legislate for the betterment and welfare of the struggling masses with the certain knowledge that prosperity will rise and further enrich those above. Those who endorse this policy and believe this program are Democrats in spite of all."

Shortly afterwards father made a personal oration to me alone, which I also took to heart. "Pet," he said, "always conduct yourself with the possibility in mind that your best friend of today may in fact become your enemy. Conduct yourself so that you will never have to be ashamed of any

144

disclosure made about you." I have tried to follow that advice.

So life went onward and upward for the Youngs, in a gradual and unhurried ascent. Those were relaxed, happy days. We moved to East Main Street and later to West Main Street, each time to a house a little bigger and better than the last one. My father was even offered a good partnership in a law firm in Cleveland. He turned it down. Home to him was Norwalk.

Meanwhile, I was playing football with the Pleasant Street Tigers (who changed my nickname from "Pet" to "Pat"), getting by in public school, worshiping the Horatio Alger hero who lifted himself by his well-known bootstraps, and going on Sundays to Presbyterian Sunday school. Norwalk, the "Maple City," in summer was green and sleepy and hot. We would move to our vacation place on the lakeshore, a thirty-five acre farm. There I picked strawberries and worked around the yard and swam in Lake Erie. Life was easy, placid and wholesome. There always seemed to be enough room and enough time.

But when the time came for me to enter Norwalk High School, I came down with inflammatory rheumatism and had to give up the swimming and football for a long while. I missed most of my first year and had to make up work, about which I began to be quite serious. Later I organized our school paper, *The Undergraduate*, and was its editor. For a while I thought I would rather be a writer than a lawyer. My greatest accomplishment of the period was an incomparable short story entitled "The Bride from Mars." Somehow, no magazine editor ever saw eye to eye with me about that manuscript. But I did sell a piece called "Imperialism—the American Crime," to a worthier publication, *Watson's Magazine*. (The editor, anticipating my own career, later became a United States Senator.)

I also wrote an editorial against Judson Harmon, the

145

governor of Ohio, who aspired to be Presidential nominee of the Democratic party. The chairman, or boss, of the county Democratic organization, Bill Kiefer, denounced me. It seems that Democratic party bosses for some reason or other very definitely did not go for me right from the start, and this has continued over the years.

My biggest rival in Norwalk High School was a friend named Arthur F. Young. (No relation.) He was always ahead of me. No matter what marks I made, he would make higher ones. My rivalry with this namesake came to a head when, encouraged by my parents, I set out one year to win the school oratory contest.

My parents sat smiling complacently among the onlookers. The title of my speech, which I had learned by heart, was "The Darker Side." It had marvelous purple passages and I had practiced its delivery before a mirror in my bedroom. The high school auditorium was crowded. There were other entries, but nearly everybody expected Art Young to win. The judges almost immediately and unanimously declared me the winner.

Then a few weeks later I went to the Northwestern Ohio High School Oratorical Contest at Bowling Green as representative of Norwalk High School. Many times since I have addressed audiences in Bowling Green, which is only some seventy miles distant from my home. It seemed like a long journey that day; I'd never been so far from home. Early in the evening when the program commenced and I was called on, I thought I was going great guns. I really could feel the audience with me, listening intently. Suddenly, I forgot the balance of my speech. I returned home one of the losers. I have lost on other occasions since then but I've probably never taken it so hard.

By the time I graduated from high school, I had turned into a pretty serious and ambitious fellow. I set out for

146

Gambier, Ohio—a mighty journey of 150 miles—to start my years at Kenyon College with a set determination to do the Youngs proud.

I had always pictured myself, like my idol Horatio, dauntless in the face of destiny, striding past obstacles, a giant in Lilliput, but my first day in college reduced me to a homesick midget. I found myself struggling with my own shyness, a handicap that had never interfered with the career of my hero, but stymied mine throughout my teens. It prevented me from making many friends in college. Learning to give the gladhand was never a part of my training for politics.

Even so, I got into a fraternity—Delta Kappa Epsilon—and the most popular fellow on the campus, a chap named Bill Bland, took an interest in me. Bill Bland was from a famous Missouri family of that name. If you had asked anyone then, it was Bill Bland you'd be told might wind up a U.S. Senator, not Steve Young. He might have, too, but he was killed in the First World War.

Like most of the students at Kenyon, I was to be found more often at beer parties than in the study hall. While Bill Bland studied, I hung around the football crowd, hoping to become a member of the team. I never did. Despite my laziness as a student, I fared well enough in the classroom, especially in economics and all the English courses, though I was terrible in subjects like chemistry and physics. At Kenyon College I began to get a glimmer of the ingredients that go into success. The president was an Episcopal minister and scholar named Dr. Pierce. Pierce, however, was careful not to emphasize the scholarly side of his personality. He concentrated on securing endowments. Success, it seemed, came to those with a knack for public relations.

I began to find myself at Kenyon when I joined the debating society and learned how to talk in public without the self-consciousness that can leave an orator paralyzed by

147

stage fright, without a word in his head. With practice I learned I could sway listeners to my viewpoint, provided I spoke out of honest conviction.

I began to be a better student about that time and when I left Kenyon College to matriculate at Adelbert College and Western Reserve University Law School in Cleveland, I had well-defined ideas about the career I would seek and some of the changes I wanted to help bring about in the world.

During the early months of my attendance at Western Reserve I regarded Cleveland as a hostile and wicked metropolis; I relaxed only when I got home. At the same time, I began to take an interest in the politics of Norwalk. My brothers had already entered the law and were partners in a firm called, appropriately, Young and Young. When Don John ran for prosecuting attorney, I wrote the motto for his campaign: "The same deal for the rich who rob the poor as for the poor who rob the rich." When I was home I started working for the Huron County *News*, the paper that had printed my notorious editorial, and managed to bring the Democrats down on my head a few more times.

When I returned to Cleveland I tried to enjoy life in the big town more thoroughly. The longer I lived in Cleveland, the better I liked it. I was taken into the law school fraternity—Phi Delta Phi. There were dances and dates and excursions to Little Italy, just a short distance from the university.

Cleveland in those days was a notably stable community in the midst of one of the most stable periods in American history. It was residential and spacious, a tranquil and beautiful city. Only later did I remember in retrospect that this city too had its full share of ugliness, its inequities, its disgraces, its crime and its slums. Cleveland was residential, but it was also a major industrial city and the worker had no protection whatsoever in case his wages suddenly stopped. A single accident to the man of the family could mean

148

tragedy. There were no unions, no workmen's compensation, and an injury might easily mean immediate descent for a family from modest comfort to total destitution. We students seldom considered these things.

At the same time, as I remember it, we had little sense of class distinction. One of the boys in our class, from a modest background, was going out with the daughter of a steel magnate. None of us found this remarkable. I, myself, had by this time met Ruby Dawley, and promptly stopped dating all other girls.

I would call for Ruby in my smartest college clothes—peg-top trousers, a long coat, high collar, wide tie. We'd go to the Old Colonial Theatre or to the opera house, or to informal dances. I wrote long, mushy letters to her. It was an unusual courtship for the period. Long before the regular quota of boxes of candy and bouquets had been delivered, not to mention the stilted speeches about the state of one's heart, culled from Victorian novels—in a total of less than three weeks Ruby and I sealed our engagement. I used to send her special delivery letters, which would enrage her father since they'd always be delivered in the middle of the night.

The thought of Ruby, of my impending marriage to that lovely girl with the copper-colored hair and the keen blue eyes, inspired me to study furiously for the bar examinations, even though my law school class was not scheduled to take them until June. However, in those days it was not required of a law student to have his law degree before taking the bar examination, though it was customary. I left Cleveland for Columbus for a few days in December, telling my classmates I was going home to have some dental work done. Actually, I was going to take the examinations.

All the way down on the train I kept cramming for those exams. I didn't have a hotel reservation but managed to find a room for the two days it took to get through the tests. I had, however, shown the foresight to send my credentials ahead of time. Later I studied for and was given the degree of LL.B.

I went back to school and waited anxiously for news from Columbus. If I failed, it would mean waiting until June to take the tests again. But I didn't fail. On January 11, 1911, I was sworn in as a lawyer. I quit the fraternity house and married Ruby Dawley. When we returned from a Niagara Falls honeymoon I tried tutoring, writing, anything to make ends meet, but couldn't make a go of it. Then I took my bride home to my parents in Norwalk.

I commenced to practice law in Norwalk and, with the help of my father and mother and in association with my brothers, the prospects were good for at least moderate success. However, I did not remain much longer in Norwalk. My wife wanted to move to Cleveland. I wanted to remain in Norwalk. We compromised. We moved to Cleveland. She was right, as she almost always was.

Soon afterward I tried my first case. This was in police court. My client was charged with assault and battery growing out of a saloon brawl. To my surprise and his he was found not guilty. I had won my first case. My father-in-law, Jay P. Dawley, a prominent Cleveland lawyer, encouraged and helped me. To this day I can't make up my mind whether my client was innocent or the judge took pity on me. I didn't do so well with my second case, a criminal trial involving "shooting to wound." I made the mistake of putting on a witness I hadn't consulted previously. I never did that again.

In 1910 the Thirteenth District Democratic Convention meeting in Mansfield nominated my father as Democratic candidate for Congress in that district. In fact they recessed the convention for many hours while urging him to accept the nomination. I hoped fervently that he would accept, for by this time I was myself hearing the siren call of politics. But he firmly declined to become a candidate. William

Sharp, an Elyria businessman then unknown outside of Elyria, was nominated, elected and later became United States Ambassador to France.

While at law school, I had neglected to make acquaintances in Cleveland. Had I expected to practice law in that city I would probably have tried then for a clerkship in some Cleveland law office. I attempted to overcome my disadvantages by tutoring, by attending Sunday school and church and by taking an active interest in local Democratic politics. Along about this time I acquired a habit which has more or less been with me throughout the years. I did not eat lunch, though sometimes I bought a bag of peanuts. In the diary I kept at that time I wrote, "Can I keep to this course amidst the gale that seems to sweep the billows over me and beneath this sky clouded and darkened by adversity?" This was really a rather melodramatic statement.

My father and father-in-law both helped us. I joined the twenty-second ward Democratic Club in Cleveland. I am certain I had no thought at the time of running for office, though I was an enthusiastic Democrat. I wanted to make acquaintances and friends. Every Friday evening I faithfully attended meetings of this ward club over Gottlieb Finkbeiner's saloon near the old ball park in Cleveland. I soon became secretary of the club and precinct captain. The Democratic ward leader, Jim McDonough, took a liking to me.

In the city election, I rang so many doorbells in my precinct that I persuaded just about every single eligible voter to go to the polls. Soon afterwards at a caucus of the county executive committee and ward leaders of the Democratic party, Newton D. Baker, who was mayor of Cleveland (he later became Secretary of War in Woodrow Wilson's Cabinet) placed my name in nomination as one of the thirteen Democratic candidates to run for Representative to the General Assembly of Ohio. The county convention made the

151

nomination unanimous. I worked hard that fall and attended every ward meeting I could, making speeches urging my election. Those speeches must have been very halting, sad affairs, but I put everything I had into that 1912 campaign. My motto was "God made all men, and he did not make some to crawl on hands and knees while others ride upon their backs."

The poverty I had seen in Cleveland out of the corner of my eyes in my law school days began to obsess me. I made countless speeches urging legislation to help the downtrodden. For the first time I felt involved in something that really mattered. Whether it was due to good fortune or the passion of my oratory, or a combination of both, Election Day in November 1912, brought me to a seat in the Ohio legislature at the age of twenty-two—the youngest man ever elected to the state law-making body.

The legal career of which I had dreamed before my father's roll-top desk in the Norwalk Court House had been transformed overnight into a political one. For me, entering politics meant first and foremost taking up the battle against injustice and inequality. It was to be a long battle—indeed, a full-length war.

CHAPTER 11

America in 1912 was a self-centered country. The Middle West especially was surrounded by a kind of psychological Great Wall of China. An Ohioan—William Howard Taft— sat in the White House. He was committed to carrying on the "big stick" policies of Theodore Roosevelt, who had picked him as his successor in the 1908 campaign and was busy trying to buy the confidence of Latin America through "Dollar Diplomacy." But the continent across the Atlantic seemed to the average Clevelander like a fairy-tale world where caricatures of Czars and Kaisers strutted and sputtered, stirring up Lilliputian controversies that could not conceivably threaten the peace of our great and bountiful land. With the election of Woodrow Wilson in November, these attitudes underwent sharp changes. Meanwhile, what preoccupied the liberal political mind at home was domestic justice.

In those days I was particularly interested in the rights of women who still were struggling toward emancipation. They had been winning important victories since 1848. The great numbers of women who worked for a living were cruelly exploited, with low wages and long, gruelling hours. The first bill I ever prepared for introduction and consideration was House Bill No. 13 in the General Assembly of Ohio. This was a proposed amendment to extend the eight-hour day to protect women and girls employed in "bakeries," "mercantile establishments," and hotels.

I had expected, as a matter of fact, to make a dramatic entrance into the legislature, call the attention of my colleagues to the injustice of the nine-hour day to the women of Ohio and win a prompt victory for so eminently fair a piece of legislation. Actually, although I finished the preparation of that amendment on December 31, 1912, it didn't get any real attention until my second term in the Ohio legislature in 1915. Even then a Republican representative named White introduced a bill identical to mine. The Republican majority recommended his bill and sidetracked mine. "That was a small piece of politics," I jotted in my diary, "but naturally I was as glad to vote for his bill as for my own measure, which I had introduced the first day." I doubt if those kind words to myself consoled me much, though.

My interest in women's rights was intensified by my membership in an organization called the Men's League for Equal Suffrage. The climax of my participation came during a pageant for the cause of votes for women when I found myself on stage attired in a white sheet wrapped about me toga-style, in the part of the Greek god Hermes. This outfit, and and many of the speeches I made, drew down on my head more jeers than cheers, which did not stop me from walking in the front line of suffragist parades alongside such courageous women as Harriet Taylor Upton, Elizabeth Hauser and Florence E. Allen.

Women's suffrage was only one of the many reforms I was eager to see pushed through. I wanted the bank depositor's savings to get proper government protection. I wanted to see laws on the books that would help banish vice and crime and at the same time protect the rights of those accused of wrongdoing. I wanted the Ohio working man to get the proper compensation when he was ill or injured. It amuses me now to think that these things were regarded by conservative Ohio as daring and even inflammatory notions.

Shortly after the eighteenth session of the Assembly con-

154

vened, in January 1913, I introduced a program calling for a short voting ballot to simplify the voting process. It consisted of three bills and an amendment to the constitution.

In the middle of February I was called into his office by Governor James M. Cox. The Governor was a man of remarkable courage and foresight who had taken the lead in workmen's compensation and unemployment insurance legislation. He was a great orator and had served in Congress and distinguished himself as a newspaper editor. He was nominated by the Democratic party at the end of the decade, in 1920, for President of the United States, and was one of the liberals, far ahead of his time, who influenced me in choosing liberalism as my political course.

But on this morning Governor Cox called me in to offer paternal counsel. "Young," he said, "you cannot get this Short Ballot bill through unless you are willing to divide it into three parts. Divide it that way and I will have it go through."

Later I realized that Governor Cox was trying to get me to temper idealism with a political solvent of compromise. I feared yielding to him; while perhaps insuring the conservative support necessary to pass the bill, it would have left me with only about half what I hoped to accomplish. I misunderstood; I thought he was trying to manipulate me. It seemed to me that my whole glorious proposal for a short ballot should be accepted in one glamorous package. I interpreted the Governor's kind words of advice as transparent flattery, his proposals to divide the resolution and to pass it victoriously through what he called "the gunshots of the enemy" as suspect and insincere.

"Governor," I said at last, "I can't do it. It isn't right to divide this resolution."

Governor Cox smiled. "But why should it make such a difference to you whether the resolution is divided or not?"

"That is not the point," I replied. "The people who voted for me don't care whether my resolution is passed or de-

155

feated. But they do expect me to try to do right. They expect me to hold firm to my ideas of what I believe to be right and in the best interest of the people of this state. I'm sorry, but I'm going to stand pat."

"That's perfectly all right," the Governor said soothingly, "if you feel that way." But I noticed that I was no longer particularly welcome in the executive offices.

Gradually I learned that legislation is largely a matter of compromise. I learned that you have to get along with your colleagues—but at the same time must firmly reject the blandishments and pressures of groups seeking special privileges and advantages. Pressure of this kind was put upon me as soon as I was elected, and it has never let up. I have never let up resisting it, either. Sometimes the firmness required can be debilitating. But it is always important to resist.

I remember my astonishment back in 1913 when lobbyists who were former state representatives would come right on the floor of the House of Representatives and try to order us about. I hadn't expected this at all. When lobbyists from the Cleveland Chamber of Commerce or the real estate board would try to get me to go to lunch to "talk things over," I decided, as I did in later years, that I was just not hungry. Sometimes, if I did go, I would insist on flipping a coin to see who would pay for the lunch. There was Robert M. Modisette who used to telephone me and write to me all the time urging me to favor his viewpoint in ways that would benefit some Ohio coal companies. The coal lobbyists, I believed, had employed him to prevail upon me to change my attitude and vote against some of Governor Cox's program, having found out somehow that we had lived at the same fraternity house at college. It didn't do them any good. I voted as I thought best and that wasn't in favor of legislation supporting the special interests of the coal companies.

We in the Eighteenth General Assembly were progressives who managed, despite all pressures, to put through legislation that improved the lot of the average Ohioan. One of the first laws passed in this country calling for workmen's compensation was ours. We passed other laws that helped to improve working conditions. We instituted prison reforms. We adjusted unfair taxation provisions. We put through bills to protect bank depositors.

I did not run for state representative entirely out of idealism. Ruby and I had been in despair over having to accept help from my parents and from her father. The salary of 1,000 dollars a year had looked mighty good to me when my net earnings from my first year of law practice amounted to little more that 700 dollars and I had to tutor high school subjects to supplement my income. When you are that hard-pressed even a minor setback looms up like a tragedy. I remember a day when my wife had gone down to the Sheriff Street Fish Market in Cleveland in order to save money and got caught in a rainstorm. This fish she had bought so cheaply soaked through the package and ruined her suit. It was her best suit of those remaining in her wardrobe from before we were married. She saw a grey-checked number in the window of a Cleveland department store, the William Taylor and Son Company, and dreamed about buying it for so long that I finally told her to go ahead and charge it to me. The price was twenty-five dollars, much less than the value of some of her clothes predating our marriage. The store refused to deliver the suit or permit me to pick it up. An officious clerk stated that I had no credit. We never dealt with Taylor's again, and I expressed no regret when they went out of business a few years ago.

Now, on 1,000 dollars a year, with my attendance at the General Assembly required for only a few months in the two-year term, Ruby and I felt like prosperous citizens with a real place in the scheme of things. On April 24, 1912, Stephen M. Young, III, had joined the family. He, too, seemed to be flourishing. I used to wake up in the morning and congratulate myself on being alive in the second decade of the twentieth century—father, husband and legislator for the state—when all the world's problems were about to be solved in gradual stages through the peaceful processes of legislation and reform, with no violence, no bloodshed and no warfare. Those were happy, relaxed days which may never return in our lifetime. That the population of our country was only 6 percent of the world's and that a majority of people everywhere existed in squalor, misery and hunger was something we either did not know or at least gave no thought to.

One of my heroes was Newton D. Baker, the mayor of Cleveland. Baker had nominated me for office. I am about five feet eight inches myself, and he was shorter than I, but he gave the impression of being a big man in every way. He was an intellectual giant and already was beginning to acquire a national reputation as a scholar and a statesman. He was the real leader of the Democrats. (Burr Gongwer, an insurance salesman, occupied no official position but was the party boss.) Later, as a key man under Wilson, Baker was to become a figure of international significance when he fought for the establishment of the League of Nations. Everyone in Cleveland should have loved Mayor Baker for the era of good government he brought to our city. But, of course, not everyone did.

Cleveland, compared to Chicago and other large American cities, was quite a God-fearing town. Even so, Billy Sunday, the Evangelist (he was a much cruder fellow than the latter-day emulators of his methods like Billy Graham), saw fit to denounce Mayor Baker and his administration as godless. When Billy Sunday came to Ohio to make converts, State Representative Martin L. Sweeney cooked up a plan with the other Cuyahoga County representatives to walk out on Sunday when he appeared before the legislature in Columbus. Twelve of the thirteen did walk out. The one who didn't was myself. Instead, I found myself rising to my feet and

158

declaring, "This is not right. Any prayer if sincerely given should be heeded." Sweeney grabbed my arm. He tried to haul me from my seat in the chamber. "Don't honor that lying trouble-maker, Sunday," he said. I shook him off. It was a matter of some weeks before Martin Sweeney could bring himself to pass the time of day with me.

I could have run for Congress as early as 1914. My aspirations were simpler and more modest, however. For one thing, I wanted a home of my own. When the legislature was not in session, Ruby and I used to take a trolley car from Cleveland to visit my parents in Norwalk or at their summer farm at Ruggles Beach. My mother was always slipping us ten-dollar bills to help us make out. An Ohio Assemblyman was not overpaid in those years.

When there was talk of my nomination as Congressman from the newly created Twenty-second District, I went to my friend, Senator Carl Friebolin, and asked him to put a stop to it. I told him I was trying to raise enough money to build a home of my own for my family in Ohio.

"I can't do that and afford the luxury of a Congressional campaign," I told him. "If I have to run for anything, I'd rather it be for a second term in the legislature."

And that is what I did. I was re-elected by a large majority this time, Cuyahoga County having gone Democratic. The legislature as a whole, however, had gone Republican, two to one. There were ninety-six Republicans, forty-eight Democrats, and one fellow—Pat O. Shank of Medina County—who described himself in the Assembly records as a "Progressive."

Elected, too, were a number of medical men: six doctors, three of them Republicans, the other three Democrats, assuring emergency treatment to all members regardless of party affiliation. And I remember I was struck by the name of one representative to that legislature from Williams County—a Mr. Frank M. Money (Republican, naturally).

159

Wilson's election to the White House in 1912—the Democratic boss of Huron County rebuked me when I lined up in favor of Wilson and stumped for his election—had opened an era of high principles. Under the banner of what he called "the New Freedom" he concentrated at first on domestic reform. Such laws as the Federal Reserve Act and the Clayton Anti-trust Act, designed to break up monopolies and restore competition to American industry, were passed at his insistence. At the same time, he maintained the American policy of strict neutrality where European affairs were concerned.

Our General Assembly in Ohio reflected the Wilsonian mood of reform at home. I remember even introducing a bill to stiffen divorce laws "to the end that there would be less tearing asunder of families." In July of 1915 my own family was increased by the arrival of Majorie Louise Young. On account of President Wilson's decision to intervene in the affairs of Mexico I didn't see as much of her at first as I might have.

Revolutions and counter-revolutions were the order of the day in the land below the border and President Wilson had recently ordered drastic action against Victoriano Huerta of Mexico for refusing to honor the American flag. (Actually, Wilson had a great deal more than that against Huerta. The new Mexican president had overthrown Francisco Madera and assassinated him and was heading up a lawless regime favored by the foreign oil, mining, railroad and land-owning interests.) When Huerta arrested some American sailors at Tampico, Wilson sent marines to Vera Cruz and mobilized the National Guard. In a burst of patriotic fervor, I enlisted in the Cleveland Grays, which had always been pretty much of a social organization, traditionally marching in inaugural parades in Washington every four years and parading in Cleveland annually on George Washington's birthday. Lately it had been turned into Company F of the Third Ohio Infantry. I remember leaving home so early in the morning that it was still dark. Ruby was downstairs in the little home we had purchased, holding our baby daughter in her arms and crying. Looking back, I feel that I was a very thoughtless husband and father indeed.

The war clouds blew away, though, and with them the prospect of active service. I found myself no farther away from home than Columbus, drilling and hiking, as far from Mexico as I had ever been. I was smitten by a feeling of futility, of time wasted. I had endured separation from my wife, my son, my new-born daughter—not to mention my own law career—and I hadn't even learned the rudiments of military training. I decided I would get some real training before I put away my uniform.

On August 8, 1916, I was nominated for Congress, without opposition, by the Democrats of the Twenty-second District. But September found me in El Paso after a four-day journey, very remote from the nearest Ohio rally or Democratic club meeting. There followed a month of drilling, hiking and rifle range practice. The Secretary of War had issued a regulation that married men in the National Guard were to be discharged upon application and Ruby had properly been exerting pressure on me to take advantage of it. I applied for a discharge, which was immediately granted. I returned to Cleveland to resume what law practice I had left and to attend to my Congressional campaign, which had been slowly dying. My campaign cost me about one hundred dollars. I was defeated in a rather close election by the Republican incumbent, H. I. Emerson. I think I should have won it even in a Republican district but I knew nothing about campaigning.

In 1917 I was offered an appointment as assistant prosecuting attorney of Cuyahoga County under the newly elected prosecuting attorney, Samuel Doerfler. The appointment was made on January 1st and then, on January 2nd, I was for one day, strictly speaking, a private citizen—away, as it were, from the public trough. Next day I started on my first case as assistant prosecutor. I was actually second assistant in the conduct of criminal cases.

I won my first case before the month of January was out. In 1917 I tried 218 felony cases and in these 160 defendants were found guilty, forty-eight were acquitted, and in ten cases the jury disagreed. The criminal cases I tried included murder, manslaughter, robbery, burglary, rape, shooting to kill, house-breaking and other crimes. No assistant prosecuting attorney in Cuyahoga County has ever since that time tried so many felony cases before a jury as I disposed of during 1917. For one thing, there was an enormous backlog of criminal cases so we worked right through the summer. While one jury was out I would save time by impaneling another jury to try another criminal case.

At last the days of scraping and scrounging, of having to accept discreet little gifts from my parents, were at an end. On a salary that was really good for those days—about 3,000 dollars a year—I was able to provide decently for myself and my family. We lived in a good house on the east side of Cleveland. In court the air might be poisoned with bitter words, charges and counter-charges, conflict and sordid disclosures; home meant peace and tranquility. Those were good years.

I was not always easy in my mind as a prosecutor. I hated injustice, but one man surrounded by the law always looked so helpless. I found it hard to get used to the idea that it was up to me to demand punishment for the guilty. Many times wives, children and mothers of men I had convicted before juries or judges pleaded with me to recommend mercy. I did this in only a few instances. Emotional considerations can't permit us to take the bandages off the eyes of justice. I learned early to urge a judge to pass on the motion for a new

162

trial without delay following conviction of a defendant. Prompt decision and sentencing saved heartaches. I do not believe that the guilty should escape punishment, or that criminals should be coddled. What depressed me as a prosecutor was that the innocent suffer with and for the guilty.

Since man is so fallible, I have never believed that anyone should take it upon himself to snuff out the life of any fellow being. I remember a boy named Thomas Gerak, who was charged with murder in the first degree. He was about seventeen, but the killing of which he'd been accused was particularly shocking. It involved shooting down a night watchman in Cleveland in the course of a robbery. The Cleveland police and the county detective wanted Gerak executed for murder. In impaneling the jury I purposely refrained from asking prospective jurors whether they were or were not opposed to capital punishment. He was convicted with the jury recommending mercy. He was sentenced to life imprisonment. Good behavior, as often happens, got Gerak released after some twenty-five years. He came to see me. I didn't recognize him until he reminded me that I had saved him from death. He never got into another bit of trouble throughout his life. There were other instances like that.

In 1916, with the slogan "He kept us out of war" plastered everywhere, Wilson was re-elected as a peace candidate, but his attempts to mediate between the warring nations were in vain. In 1917, when the Germans resumed unrestricted submarine warfare, he had little choice but to bring us into the war "to make the world safe for democracy." As a married man with two children and as a public official I was exempt from the draft, but I waived exemption.

The country had turned its mind to the affairs of Europe now, perhaps with more fervor than reasoned concern, and this wave of patriotism affected me as it did my friends and family. I wrote in my diary, "I desire very much to join the army and render a real and needful service on the firing line."

It never came to that. Ruby didn't want me to enlist. I kept on working as assistant prosecutor.

In 1918 I was prosecuting a girl named Elsie Bass who was accused in a milk poisoning case. I obtained a conviction for manslaughter. After that, I didn't want to try any more cases for a while. I wanted to be in Europe where it seemed to me injustice was raging on a far larger scale.

I went to Chicago to apply for a commission in the Chemical Warfare Branch of the Army. I was turned down. I wrote to Newton D. Baker, who was Secretary of War, seeking a commission. Again I was turned down; I don't think Baker saw my letter. At last an application I made to the Field Artillery Officers Training School at Camp Zachary Taylor in Kentucky was approved.

Shortly before I left for Camp Zachary Taylor I listened to a lecture in the Cleveland auditorium given by some major general who knew all the answers. Austria, by this time, had sued for a separate peace, but the major general asserted the war was going to last at least seven years longer! If this know-it-all had said seven weeks he would have been closer to the truth, so I didn't get any nearer to the front in that war than Camp Zachary Taylor, Kentucky. And I didn't do too well there. No matter how neatly I folded my blankets or how many times I cleaned my quarters I couldn't seem to satisfy the sergeants who were so fond of throwing their weight around. I was an officer candidate when I went to Camp Zachary Taylor and I was an officer candidate when the Armistice came in 1918, but it was 1919 when I finally got back to civilian life.

When I got home I was re-appointed assistant county prosecuting attorney. Miss Cusick, the stenographer in my office, greeted me on my return with what she called a lovely surprise. By some mistake my salary had been coming through during the four months I had been away. I returned the checks to the county auditor. Later in 1919 I became chief criminal prosecuting attorney in charge of the criminal branch of that office. I discovered that Florence E. Allen, whom I had met in the Men's League for Equal Suffrage years before, was struggling along in a small law office. I appointed her one of my assistants, the first woman prosecuting attorney in the United States. The Democratic party boss, Burr Gongwer, didn't want her appointed. But I talked it over with Mrs. Bernice Pyke, a leader of the Democratic women in Cuyahoga County and, in fact, the leading Democratic woman in our state, who persuaded Gongwer to relent. I put Miss Allen on the Grand Jury to hear proceedings at first. Later she tried felony cases, reaching all the way from first degree murder down. She was a highly intelligent young woman and an excellent speaker. She has always been a great lady. Before long she went on to be a Common Pleas judge, then a judge of the Ohio Supreme Court, a United States District Court judge, later a judge of the United States Circuit Court of Appeals. She recently retired. At one time she was considered for an appointment to the United States Supreme Court by President Franklin D. Roosevelt.

Miss Allen, who never married, holds me responsible for the only drink she ever took. It was at our house on an evening when wine was served with dinner. She had a tiny glass —just one—but that was a debauch for her.

Only once as chief prosecutor was I offered a bribe. It wasn't a particularly big one. A washerwoman came to me on Christmas Eve to plead for her son, whose probation report was on my desk. It was his first offense—he was just a boy— and the charge was theft. He had pleaded guilty in the middle of the trial.

165

"Go easy on my boy," the woman pleaded brokenly. It was like a scene in a sentimental movie. Then she offered me a dollar.

"Thank you," I said. "Believe me, I'll go as easy as I can on your boy, but I could not take any money."

In those days, it seems to me, Ohio justice was singularly fair and impartial. Judges were more lenient, jurors more humane. Youngsters got into trouble but there wasn't the juvenile delinquency that has become a national—indeed, an international—problem today. Things are harsher now. And harsh times make harsh men.

In 1922, I was nominated for Attorney General of Ohio on the Democratic ticket. I put everything into that campaign—perhaps too much. I lashed out in one speech at the telephone company for charging "abnormal rates for subnormal service." A few weeks later, when the new phone books were issued, I found my name missing. I didn't wait for an explanation. I filed suit immediately. This rash act didn't further my election chances. All state candidates, including myself, were defeated by the Republicans. It was not much comfort to me that of all the defeated Democratic candidates for state office, I had come the closest to winning. My opponent was a Prohibitionist—one of the many Ohio Anti-Saloon League members who drank "wet" and voted "dry." The Drys were strong that year. I had certainly conducted a strange campaign—no manager, no plans. I just went to meetings and shook hands. This technique was futile against the cry of the hour: "Back to normalcy and the full dinner pail."

My own route to "normalcy" was back to private law. I headed my own firm in partnership with Kent H. Meyers— Young and Meyers. Business was good.

The only really shattering thing that happened to me all during the decade of the twenties was my father's death from cancer in 1922. He had worked actively as Common

166

Pleas judge right up to a month or so before his death. In my book he was a great father and a great man.

Otherwise, the busy years slipped by. I never entirely got over being a prosecuting attorney, although I defended many criminal cases. I had to turn down some and I took on some without fee—particularly cases where defendants were charged with violations of the prohibition laws.

The twenties were tranquil times for us. Those years are always described as being brimful of sin, wild drinking, high living, but there wasn't much of that in Cleveland. We had night clubs, but if they were speakeasies I never knew it. At least, I never had to give the password to some tough guy in back of a grill in order to drink bathtub gin in a shadowy basement.

We may have avoided the highjinks of the twenties in Ohio, but we didn't avoid retribution for the big boom. The depression struck Ohio with terrible force. There was hunger and hardship everywhere. There were soup kitchens and bread lines in Cleveland. There were runs on banks, as there were everywhere. I witnessed a frightening run on the Guardian Trust Company in which I was a depositor. Years later I believe I received five cents on the dollar on my savings. I lost all the money I had saved or invested, but some of my friends suffered far greater losses. A few took their lives.

In 1931 Governor George White appointed me to the Ohio Commission on Unemployment Insurance. We held hearings in 1931 in various Ohio cities. I helped draft the commission's report recommending that Ohio adopt unemployment insurance. Also I helped write the first unemployment insurance law. We were pioneers in that.

The 1930 census gave Ohio two additional Congressmen. The General Assembly did not redistrict for Congressional purposes, so the two were to be elected at large. The county Democratic boss, who was still Burr Gongwer, didn't support me. But I made an intensive campaign and was nominated. Charles V. Truax, a former Ohio director of agriculture, was nominated along with me.

There were five candidates for the Democratic nomination. When I won the nomination I started working for election on a person-to-person level. I went from town to town. I went to every meeting where I was welcome and to some where I was not. I had no financing. I had no campaign manager. I would go to a picnic or a rally or a parlor, wherever a meeting was held, big or small, near or far. When I look back on my campaign for Congressman-at-large, I believe I might have been elected six times instead of four had I really made adequate campaigns and perhaps raised a few thousand dollars each time in campaign contributions. The thought of doing this never occurred to me. A prominent Ohio Democratic state central committeeman named William Durbin supported me. However, he sent me a letter once rapping me for denouncing the Ku Klux Klan in an Ohio city, Napoleon. I called them unprincipled "pillow slip knights." "I think the same as you about these fellows in the hoods, but there are some things we don't talk about," he wrote. Unfortunately, there are still many people who would like everybody to keep a tactful silence while evil men and women use the backs of their neighbors as steps up to power.

Wherever I went in the course of my campaign I saw hungry people—frightened, worried, sick-looking, unsmiling people. I talked to groups waiting on breadlines, at soup kitchens. I said, "We need a new deal in America. I hope to be your Congressman, and help put it over. I need your vote." I denounced the fact that "thirteen million worthy and industrious men were walking city streets jobless and that farmers were not making enough money to pay interest on their mortgages and to pay their taxes." I said the entire financial structure of the United States was collapsing and that our Republican President, Herbert Hoover, did nothing

168

but pull the covers over his head, shiver and repeat that "prosperity was just around the corner."

When Franklin D. Roosevelt came to Ohio, I rode on the campaign train with him. He wished me luck. I already admired him, but that radiant smile, turned on *me* personally, reinforced my respect, admiration and affection. I was sure even then that he was a man who would do great things to restore the strength and stability of this country. And I wanted to be in Washington to help him.

One of my opponents was George H. Bender of Cleveland, a blustering, shrewd, outspoken Republican politican. He ran against me not only that year but every succeeding year when I was up for election as Congressman-at-large. George H. Bender and I started out as political enemies, but we managed as the years passed to turn into personal enemies as well. My other opponent was L. T. Palmer. We had served in the armed forces together, and turned into friends. Both Palmer and Bender defended Hoover, of course, while I denounced him and his do-nothing policies.

This campaign was rough. I remember that the editor of the Cleveland *News* said I was insulting the Chief Executive of the United States. But the people of Ohio elected me as their Representative-at-large.

CHAPTER 12

✍ *Although I had been to Washington before, gaping like other tourists at the broad avenues and white buildings, although I had stood with wet eyes before the monuments of Lincoln and Jefferson and crowded my way to a slit in the Washington Monument to peer down at the breathtaking geometry of the city, I had never been there to take part in a history-making moment until one blustering day in March 1933. I was there to hear Franklin D. Roosevelt deliver his first inaugural address. I had arrived alone as a Congressman-at-large from Ohio. I sat next to a Representative from Maine newly elected, like myself, listening to the new President as he said those words that would resound through the years: "The only thing we have to fear is fear itself." I felt he was talking straight to me. I was forty-four at the time. I had been in politics for years. But the prospect of serving my country as a Congressman representing the entire state of Ohio seemed to me an inspiring but terrifying responsibility. I needed to hear those words that counseled against fear.*

Fear stalked America. It was indeed the enemy. I can still remember the menacing clouds scudding across the sky over the Capitol. I can almost hear the whine of the March wind again. Hunger and unemployment and poverty made the mood of the whole nation dark. How much we wanted to believe Roosevelt when he said, "This great nation will endure as it has endured, will revive and will prosper." But we had been hearing for a long time that prosperity was just around the corner.

After the March 4th inaugural I went home to Cleveland. When President Roosevelt called the Congress into session for March 9th, I drove to Washington via Steubenville where I was joined by Charles V. Truax, also newly elected Congressman-at-large. Charlie actually lacked the money to pay for his transportation to the capital, so we went together to Washington.

I had a room waiting for me at the Raleigh Hotel on the night of March 8th and I tried to go to sleep in that unfamiliar place. I was going to be sworn in as a Congressman the next morning and I wanted to start that big day in my life feeling well and rested. I could not sleep. I was too excited. And, despite the President's words about fear, I felt afraid—afraid for all the millions of hungry and bewildered and worried people in the land. Afraid I would let them, and myself, down. What if this new administration of which I was to be a part failed to turn the tide in the nation's economy? I couldn't stop thinking about an eleven-year-old boy, the son of a couple I knew, who had hanged himself because his parents, out of hunger, had killed his pet rabbit and the family had eaten it.

At the same time I felt elated. I was looking forward to the 10,000-dollar a year salary I was about to start collecting —not knowing yet that one of the first bills the President would get through was the so-called Economy Act which would bring that 10,000 dollars down to 8,500. Even that was a lot of money in those days.

I got up about six in the morning on March 9th, leaving the hotel at seven to walk through the shivery streets looking for a place to have breakfast. I finally stopped at Thompson's Cafeteria. Then I went over on the Navy Yard streetcar to the House of Representatives. I was eager to get a look at the office assigned to me.

172

I found the place occupied by a Congressman on the Ways and Means Committee who had been beaten unexpectedly in the election and who said he just hadn't had enough time to move out. I said I understood and let his staff set me up at a stenographer's desk in a corner. Three weeks later he finally moved out and I got the office to myself. He must have been a slow packer.

I was happy to see there was some mail for me already—mainly letters and telegrams from friends and well-wishers. A little later I went over with Charles Truax to see the sergeant-at-arms in the House of Representatives. Our business was urgent. We borrowed against our first pay checks.

Later I put on my overcoat and went for a walk around the plaza in the Capitol. I tried to get out of my mind the boy who hanged himself because of the rabbit. I recalled what President Willard of the Baltimore and Ohio Railroad had said not long before, that if his family was hungry he would steal. I continued to think of those thirteen million Americans out of work. I looked at the classical architecture, the broad lawns, the monuments looking as though they had been built to endure forever. I thought of the bright young men just out of universities, their futures dim, and how they were beginning to question all our institutions. Those of them who obtained jobs at fifteen or twenty-five dollars a week were lucky. Then once more a mood of exaltation stole over me. I had been elected by the people of my state to do something towards abolishing poverty and injustice and to help put America back on the tracks to greatness. Seventy-two years after George Washington came Abraham Lincoln. Now another seventy-two years had gone by. Maybe the Almighty had put the finger on FDR to lead the country out of trouble in its time of despair. Being a politician, I didn't let that thought go by unexploited. I used it later in a speech.

At noon we were to be sworn in, but first there was a

173

Democratic caucus in the caucus room. There were several candidates for Speaker of the House, and their backers were pushing the favorites. One Ohio Representative, Robert Crosser, wanted the votes of the whole delegation. He had no chance whatsoever to be Speaker, but he wanted the votes anyway. Henry T. Rainey of Illinois, who appeared to be the leading candidate, was a prospect close to my heart; I found myself standing up and speaking out for him. Not yet sworn in, and already making speeches! I was to hear some disapproving comments later about my temerity. Yet I felt that I had a right to speak up, and I'd probably do it all over again the same way, given the same circumstances. And Rainey did actually become Speaker of the House for the Seventy-third Congress. Congressman Crosser received no votes in the Democratic caucus except a few from Ohio. He never forgave me for my refusal to support him.

Now the morning was over and it was time for the swearing in. The walls of this venerable chamber had been looking down on Congressmen since 1857. The benches stretch in a great semi-circle divided by seven aisles. One of these desks would be mine—one out of 435. Overhead were the state seals painted on the glass panels of the ceiling. We moved toward the rostrum behind which hung the solemn rectangle of our flag. The galleries were filled. Speaker of the House Henry T. Rainey administered the oath to all of us at once—not individually, the way they do it in the Senate. I remember that oath:

"I do solemnly swear that I will support and defend the Constitution of the United States against all enemies, foreign and domestic; that I will bear true and faithful allegiance to the same; and that I take this obligation freely without any mental reservation or purpose of evasion, and that I will well and faithfully discharge the duties of the office which I am about to enter. So help me God."

174

I took the words seriously. I wanted to get to work. I didn't even stop for lunch.

My office, with its "former" occupant still very much in it, was on the first floor of the Old House Office Building. When I got back there I noticed a sight I had been reading about in the papers, but hadn't expected to see from my own window—the "Bonus Army" camped on the Capitol grounds. This ragged group of veterans had come to Washington the year before demanding help from President Hoover; what they got was tear gas and the threat of bayonets. The late General Douglas MacArthur was then in command of our Army. He turned the might of the real Army on the "Bonus Army" and their wives and children. They were unarmed. Their tents and some of their meager provisions were burned. The Chief of Staff on the scene was Lieutenant Colonel Dwight Eisenhower. The remnants of the "Bonus Army" stayed at Anacostia Flats near the Capitol to see what the new Administration would do for them. I watched these war veterans, many with their wives and children, in the fields close to the House Office Building cooking their food over cans of Sterno. Suddenly I heard a familiar voice addressing them. It was my colleague Truax. "You offered your lives as sacrifices on the altars of freedom," he was saying, "and now the least we can do for you is give you this bonus."

Later I voted against the soldiers' bonus. I didn't object to the veterans coming to Washington and petitioning Congress, but I had strong doubts as to their claim at a time when funds were so low. After listening to Truax address the veterans for a while, I turned from the window and sat down at my cramped stenographer's desk. I tried to organize a few things. Irene Hopkins, my secretary from Cleveland, had arrived and I dictated some letters. (I had to find another stenographer's desk for her to work at.) I talked to other applicants for stenographers' jobs. While I was doing

175

this one of my colleagues from Ohio asked me to put his daughter on my payroll at 2,400 dollars a year while she actually worked for him. He offered to put "anybody I wanted" on his payroll at the same salary. I said no.

I wrote a long handwritten letter to my wife in Cleveland and, before the day was over, I hired a girl named Elsie Prefitt. Elsie was so eager for a job she offered to work for fifty-five dollars a month. She got a bit more than that. She earned much more than she received.

That first afternoon as a Congressman I also had my first encounter with federal lobbyists. I found them much bolder than the state lobbyists. There was one group who wanted me to fight a bill which they said would "reduce salaries." I was startled. "Salaries?" I must have gone a little pale. "Yes," their spokesman replied, "maybe even Congressmen's salaries." They left me a bit shaken.

There was also another group, a bevy of anti-vivisection ladies who barged in around 5:30 p.m. demanding immediate action on the matter of vivisecting livestock, the cruelty and inhumanity of which they made extremely graphic. Since they were from Illinois, I tried to persuade them to go see their own Congressman, but they said I represented them, too, and they would see all the Congressmen they pleased, no matter how busy, since their mission must take priority.

It was a long day. When it was over I took some papers to the Raleigh where they were glad to have me as a guest for seventy-five dollars a month. I called my wife and asked her how she was and how the children were. When I hung up I felt terribly alone. Nobody so far had invited me to any glamorous Washington parties. I started to study the rules of the House of Representatives. I didn't even go to the movies, which I like to do. I just wanted to learn the ground rules of my new job and get some sleep so I could face the next day.

176

CHAPTER 13

I once talked to a college man who had never read the Constitution of the United States. If, like him, you have never read it—or haven't for a long time—you may, upon re-reading it, experience at least one surprise. Our Constitution does not commence with the powers and duties of the President. It does not begin with a reference to the Supreme Court. First mention goes to the House of Representatives.

That order of things did not happen accidentally. The makers of our Constitution deliberately and solemnly planned it that way. The patriot fathers had experienced the tyranny of an English king. They mistrusted rulers. They had their doubts about the Senate, feeling it might become another English House of Lords. But they trusted the House of Representatives and so they specifically gave to the House of Representatives its mighty powers—control of the purse strings, the power to tax and the sole power of impeachment. They then provided that every Representative must go home and submit his record to the people who elected him for approval at the end of every two years. Thus, the House of Representatives belongs particularly to the common man. It is the heart and soul of our democracy. It is a true cross-section of the American people.

I had come to Washington from Ohio as an earnest, if not totally innocent legislator from the Middle West, with an honest interest in doing the job the people of my state had elected me to do—and I was but one of 435 men who sat in the House trying to turn the New Deal from campaign promises into a nation-wide reality.

As it turned out, one of my first speeches was a plea to cut, among other things, my own salary. "Mr. Speaker," I said, "we are confronted by stern realities. We deal with a condition, not a theory. Not since the Federal troops streamed back to Washington in 1861 has our government been so menaced and shaken as at present. No member of this legislative body witnessed in his lifetime a more perilous time in his country's affairs than he beheld before our President was inaugurated . . . " I urged my fellow Congressmen to uphold the President's leadership and to vote for the drastic economy bill he had sent for our consideration. I know I did not speak persuasively, but others did, and our salaries were reduced to 8,500 dollars per year.

What the Congress had to face was little less than national chaos. The entire financial structure of the country had collapsed. Banks in forty-eight states were closed. Prohibitive tariffs approved by President Hoover had crippled our international trade. Transportation was paralyzed. Factories were shut down. The farmers were bankrupt—in Ohio many were ready to revolt. Millions of industrious men and women walked city streets, jobless. Millions of children were underfed. I myself had watched the savings of some of the best years of my own life disappear. I knew how it felt to be burdened by debts. People I knew and loved had taken their own lives. Our opponents called those of us who supported the Roosevelt recovery program "rubber stamp Congressmen." It was they who were the rubber stamps—counterfeit Democrats and reactionary Republicans who had always voted with Wall Street, for the public utilities, for the special interests. They supported the selfish ends of powerful people intent on getting theirs. We who supported Roosevelt be-

178

lieved he had a mandate from the people and was working to provide for the general welfare.

Once, in a speech before a county Democratic central committee, when I was up for re-election at the end of my first term, I said, "No major political party will ever challenge the basic reforms which the administration has written into law." Hindsight makes prophets of us all, but I seem to have predicted correctly on that occasion. Who can imagine a candidate for President of this country getting into the White House today on a platform advocating the repeal of social security, minimum wage laws, protection of bank deposits, collective bargaining? Let him try.

I did not always go along with Roosevelt. I liked then, as now, to do my own thinking. Roosevelt's personal charm and persuasiveness do not need additional testimony from me, but I balked at some of his ideas. The Democratic party bosses in Cuyahoga County almost invariably opposed me. They called me a "loner." I have remained one.

Despite the common sense in the main outlines of the President's recovery program, it was a struggle to get it through. In my heart I felt grave doubts about the Economy Act for which I had spoken up; I wondered whether cutting down expenses would really restore prosperity. How could withdrawing money from circulation, reducing salaries in government—which might be followed by salary reductions in industry—make our economy healthy? My colleague Truax voted against the measure. I voted for it because I felt that with the entire financial structure in a state of collapse and our free institutions in jeopardy, the act had more in its favor than against it, and the experiment ought at least to be tried.

The student who attempts today to make sense out of that period is confronted with the bewildering array of abbreviations our Republican opponents were calling "alphabet soup." Imagine what it was like for us in Congress at the time! The bills came through in such bewildering succession you could hardly read them before it was time to vote on them—NRA, AAA, NYA, PWA and, later WPA, to name a few. Roosevelt made eight major speeches to Congress and guided nineteen major measures through both houses during the "hundred days." It was all so confusing that at one point I suggested we might combine all these agencies and call the whole thing simply "IOU." There was one combination of letters, however, which did not stand for any relief agency— G. O. P.

During this period I got my first invitation from the White House when the President called in a group of freshmen Congressmen. There were about ten of us. He had summoned us to "work his charm" on us, but it wasn't really necessary. The whole country was under that spell already.

The President passed cigarettes around. I refused. "My wife does the smoking in our family," I said. "I do the drinking." He put his arm around me and replied, "My boy, you have the better part of it."

I had already spoken up against Prohibition on the House floor. "The water wagon has met its Waterloo," I said, urging legalization of beer and opening of the breweries. "Let us have temperance instead of Prohibition!" I cried. "Let the government profit instead of the beer racketeer profiteer! Let us put America to work!" Later, when my wife joined me in Washington, she managed to get most of the exclamation points out of my speeches. The early ones were terribly dramatic.

Some months afterward the President and Mrs. Roosevelt held a formal reception for all the members of Congress. The only trouble was I didn't own a tuxedo. Ruby came down to Washington a week ahead of time and helped me to pick one out from a rental place for about five dollars. Then, on the night of the reception, I couldn't find any black oxfords.

180

The shoes I wound up wearing were tan. It didn't matter. There was such a crowd I doubt if anyone noticed whether my shoes were brown or black. I had a feeling these shoes were on Ruby's mind as we got on to the endless line where we waited to shake hands with the Roosevelts. They made a curious picture waiting there together. The President appeared to be standing, but his actual position in a reclining chair was concealed by an arrangement of ferns. Mrs. Roosevelt, standing near him, looked very tall. However, when it finally came our turn to be greeted, I forgot all about that. Being smiled at by Eleanor Roosevelt was like stepping out into the sunshine on a fine spring day. She acted as though the main event of the evening for her was precisely meeting the Congressman-at-large from Ohio and his wife. She chatted with Ruby and I heard her say, "So lovely of you to come, Mrs. Young," but in that musical voice the words sounded as though they had never been uttered before. I don't know how the Roosevelts ever endured those evenings. The line of their guests seemed endless.

Aside from the tan shoes I don't really remember too much about that night. The picture in my mind is of potted palms and glittering lights and chandeliers and hundreds of Congressmen all properly shod in black oxfords. One incident does stick in my mind. There was a table handsomely arranged with food and a big punch bowl. As I was helping myself to some of it Judge Smith of Virginia—he had traded the bench for a Congressional seat and is Chairman of the House Rules Committee today—came up and asked me if the punch tasted good. I said I thought it was just fine and filled a cup for him. He tried it, smacked his lips as if what he had tasted were very good indeed, and then almost instantly gave me a most horrified look. He said, "I am afraid there is something spirituous in that drink." There is nothing more serious than a Prohibitionist. Judge Smith's behavior was mild compared to one Anti-Saloon Leaguer who, while I was cam-

181

paigning at Zanesville, expressed his hostility to the idea of repeal by spitting in my face.

Later that year I was enjoying the first vacation I had taken since becoming a Congressman. Ruby and I were spending it on a trip to Haiti and the Canal Zone. It so happened that Judge Smith also turned up on the same boat with his wife. I don't drink much, but when he came on board, there I stood with a glass in my hand. You could read from his expression the conclusions he drew and of course my voting record on the Prohibition question proved the worst.

When I think of that year what comes to my mind is the memory mostly of plain hard work. There were so many bills to act on there wasn't even time for a single filibuster. The only time really wasted was when the Republicans, although they were hopelessly outnumbered in Congress, did what they could to obstruct the passage of New Deal bills.

We who supported the National Recovery Act did have some misgivings about the constitutionality of the NRA and some other bills, but we felt that the makers of the Constitution had legislated for 1787 and thirteen orphan states, not for all time. The courts of our country on many occasions had recognized the changes wrought by time and interpreted the law accordingly. The reaction back in Ohio to my liberal speeches was interesting. The Chamber of Commerce of Cleveland didn't seem so worried about my fervor for the New Deal as about certain specific bills which affected the interests of particular Ohio businessmen.

My old nemesis, Burr Gongwer, the party boss, was after me on the phone all the time. He had been for Roosevelt at first but then had turned against him. He used to say, in a gentle but menacing purr, "I am afraid you are going to vote wrong on this, Steve." I voted the way I planned, as usual. I remember one bill asking for an appropriation for some business that was defunct. The interests who had introduced this private bill were hoping to collect a couple of thousand dollars to pay some lawyers who had represented the company. They came to the wrong man. I believe the bill was passed, however.

The thing that I thought should concern Ohio Congressmen most was the plight of the farmers in our state. They were ready for revolt. Some groups had appeared in courtrooms to threaten Ohio judges who signed foreclosure decrees. In defense of his AAA program the President had said, "I tell you frankly it is a new and unprecedented practice, but I tell you with equal frankness that an unprecedented condition calls for a new means to renew agriculture." With cotton selling for 6 cents a pound, wheat for 30 cents a bushel, corn for 10 cents a pound, forty million farmers appealing for help with their mortgages foreclosed, homes confiscated, oppressive taxes bearing down on those seeking to struggle along, I stood up for the AAA.

I also stood up for social security, for unemployment insurance, for housing designed to make it possible for American families to live decently. I was particularly enthusiastic about the CCC, which took aimless and idle young people out of the cities and sent them to the forests and the fields, doing useful and meaningful work in helping to conserve the resources of this country. I was in favor of the WPA and I was especially in favor of the Home Owners Loan Corporation. By distributing loans to home owners of good character, it saved many people from losing everything they had.

I was a New Dealer, all right, although I balked at some things.

Nowadays people call up or write you to make appointments. Back in the depression, callers on Congressmen had a tendency just to turn up. They would stay at the YMCA, or even sleep in their cars. You would have to be pretty heartless to ignore some of those visitors. When the Home Owners Loan Corporation was set up there seemed to be an unending procession of Ohioans coming down to get help before their mortgages were foreclosed.

There were many who simply wanted work. There was even a former judge bucking for any sort of a job where he might use his legal knowledge. The next day he was serving as attorney for the Home Owners Loan Corporation in Louisville. There were hundreds of young men for whom I was able to get jobs in the CCC. There were also people who couldn't be helped, men like the one who barged into my office shouting he wanted "payment," without ever specifying for what. He got a little violent.

Then there was the mail. There must have been a thousand plots for tragic novels in the letters I got in those days. I used to come down to the office before anybody else to look those letters over. Everybody seemed to have some terrible financial problem. People didn't have time to write the kind of abusive letters to Congressmen that they do today. Once in a while I would start a crusade of my own.

In particular, I led one against the federal judges of my state and other states who were refusing to repay 15 percent of their salaries voluntarily into the United States Treasury. I read aloud in Congress the names of federal judges from Ohio who had refused to take pay cuts—Samuel H. West, Paul Jones, John H. Killits, George P. Hahn, Benson W. Hough and Robert R. Nevin, as well as U. S. Circuit Judge Smith Hickenlooper. I felt that some federal judges had usurped powers and functions not rightly theirs, and had frequently made a mockery of trial by jury. It seemed to me that they had become not public servants but public tyrants. I was shocked by their refusal to accept salary cuts in the midst of the grave national emergency and I never tired of going after them. Too often our United States judges try to be judges, prosecutors and jurors all rolled into one. They

184

have life terms in office and get exaggerated ideas of their own infallibility. Some have earned a reputation for mistreating those on trial and those who defend the defendants. Today we have more good federal judges than we had in the Roosevelt era. They used to be appointed by political bosses. The bar associations which, in a sense, are unions for lawyers, have helped improve all that.

My denunciations of federal judges didn't help me any when I came back to Ohio to practice law in later years. I would try cases before men like Judge West and receive, literally, the cold shoulder. Once he turned completely around in his swivel chair with his back toward me, obviously manifesting contempt. Despite that, I continued my argument. Almost immediately one of the jurors also turned his chair around as far as he could so that his back was toward me. I got the point. Judge West was among those I had called "judicial hogs" for failing to take 15 percent salary cuts. I lost that case; or rather my client did—for hiring the wrong lawyer.

In a more stable economic era it may seem that the rapid passage of bills in the first years of the Roosevelt administration added up to a kind of "instant legislation." Yet it could scarcely have been otherwise. After the crash of '29 the government had sat on its hands and done nothing. If every bill in Roosevelt's recovery program had been written in committee, it would have taken years to pass them all.

Roosevelt needed the powers he assumed to help bring about national recovery, but he was never a dictator as we have come to understand that ugly word. Indeed, a lot of us stood up and spoke our minds whenever we thought he was acting in a dictatorial way. There was one bill he wished passed in 1933, which would have given him the power to condemn as criminal any individual exporting arms or ammunition. We felt that if he thought the export of arms would encourage the employment of force abroad, then the power to declare the exporter a criminal should be given to Congress and not to him alone.

For the most part Americans continued to be self-centered during that period and not to concern themselves with arms shipped abroad or employed by foreign powers in aggressive acts. Hitler was on his way up and the seeds of war were being sown in Europe, but we were too busy with our own affairs to pay much attention. I was surprised, therefore, in looking over my record as Congressman-at-large to learn that I was one of the first to speak out against Hitler and his persecution of the Jews. On March 20, 1934, I said, "Persecution of the Jews by the Hitler-Nazi regime is an affront to liberty-loving people everywhere. Persecution of the Jewish people and propaganda against them tramples underfoot rationality and the equal liberties for which our forefathers fought. Our government, founded by people in search of religious liberty, should still fight on for a principle so dear to all lovers of liberty." And yet I was against barring arms to the Japanese by Presidential decree. I called the depression "worse than war," a figure of speech I would think about twice later on.

"The real enemy of the American people," I stated, commenting on the removal of the battle fleet of the United States from the Pacific to the Atlantic, "is not Japan or any foreign country. The enemies of the American people are unemployment, hunger, cold, distress and suffering. These are the enemies that we, as representatives of the people, must combat. A stranger from another planet coming into our midst, beholding a surplus of wheat and pork, and people hungry; an abundance of cotton and wool, and people inadequately clothed; plenty of coal, and people cold, would say this was an insane nation. We were, but thank God we are finding our way out." In terms of the situation as we

186

knew it then, perhaps involuntary unemployment actually *was* worse than war.

One did not need to be a flaming liberal to support President Roosevelt in his efforts to hasten this country out of the depression. That is why I voted in the Seventy-third Congress for the Economy Act to reduce compensation for officers and employers in accordance with the index figure of the cost of living. I voted for all the New Deal measures with the exception of a bill authorizing the Recovery Finance Corporation to purchase stock in an insurance company. I voted for emergency relief, especially to the farmer, for the TVA development bill, for the National Industrial Recovery Act, for the modification of tariff duties and import restrictions and for the regulation of stock exchange activities. In the years since then I have had every reason to be especially proud of the Tennesse Valley Authority and have supported every appropriation for the TVA, which was a mighty bulwark in the defense of our country throughout World War II. I doubt if we would have had an A-bomb in 1945 except for the TVA. Yet, despite my record in speaking up with my colleagues for the kind of legislation that would aid American recovery, I was opposed by the Cuyahoga County Democratic organization when my name came up for re-election.

Burr Gongwer prevailed on a charming and knowledgeable Cleveland club woman named Olive Joy Wright to run for one of the two nominations as Congressman-at-large. He proceeded then to lay down an infuriating rule that I could make no speeches in the Democratic meetings in the county unless I first urged votes for Olive Joy Wright—who was in reality my opponent! I was called to the telephone and told about this when I was in the middle of a tennis match I happened to be winning. When I came back to the court I lost the set. It seemed to me a definite omen that I was also going to lose the nomination. As primary day approached I be-

187

came increasingly gloomy over my prospects. There were two Congressmen-at-large to be nominated. They might claim that Mrs. Wright was not really running against me, but I knew that only one of us from Cleveland would win a nomination; the other nominee would be my colleague from downstate, Charlie Truax.

There were scores of meetings, and big meetings, too, in the county. When I tried to speak out for myself for the nomination and for the policies of FDR at some of these meetings, I could hardly be heard above the hoots. Still, I ignored the party bosses and continued to seek the nomination without their support.

"At the time I took my solemn oath as your Congressman," I told those who would listen, "the United States seemed doomed to collapse. A depression, first voidable, and then terminable, had been permitted by the inept and do-nothing Hoover administration to become a national calamity . . . our new President acted promptly and the Congress moved rapidly. We did not postpone the hope nor continue the hunger of unemployed and underfed men, women and children. Nineteen reconstruction measures of tremendous importance were enacted by a Congress which was devoted to the country, not as Republicans and Democrats, but as Americans. American recovery has justified this record . . . business activity in the country is increasing. The question heard everywhere is, 'At last, are we really on the way?' The answer has been made by the President and a patriotic American Congress. One hundred twenty-five million people have been led away from the threat of revolution and chaos. We are definitely on the way to a new era of prosperity, plenty and progress."

But apparently nobody was listening.

A parade of Democratic women carrying American flags down the streets of Cleveland was planned for primary night after the returns came in. This was to be a victory parade celebrating the nomination of Olive Joy Wright. My secretary late that night phoned Mrs. Pyke and asked her, "When does the parade for Olive Joy Wright begin?" Mrs. Pyke answered, "My God, lady, there isn't going to be any parade. We lost." I had come out first of five candidates. Mrs. Wright ran third.

Once again a candidate, I traveled all over Ohio, talking bread-and-butter issues and supporting the President's program. Once again, without the help of my own party leadership, I campaigned my way back into office. The rank and file members of the Democratic party were then, as they have always been, very good to me.

CHAPTER 14

✍ *A curious thing happened when the 1934 election was over. Chambers of Commerce back in Ohio were becoming violently opposed to Roosevelt. Things were good for them. Their businesses had been saved. As Roosevelt put it, "I saved them from drowning and now they complain because they have lost their top hats." They called us socialists. But projects like the Tennessee Valley Authority benefited the independent, rugged individualist farmers and their wives more than anyone else. Rural electrification spared the farmers' wives grueling hard labor. Before the bills connected with it had passed through Congress, only about 8 percent of the farm families of my home state had electricity. But selfish interests, having received their transfusions of life-saving aid from the government, were showing the cantankerous symptoms of convalescence.*

New terms are invented to identify our right-wingers. Today we call them "the radical right." In the thirties they were called Coughlinites and Townsendites. It is merely a matter of semantics. Like the rich, the right wing is always with us to turn back the clock and to lead the people back into the dark ages by appealing to instincts of selfishness, intolerance and hostility. In the mid-thirties we had Father Charles Coughlin, a Catholic priest from Detroit who could frighten a radio listener out of a year's growth from two rooms away. He had started out by supporting Roosevelt and the New Deal because he hated Hoover and bankers. Now he said he wanted to abolish private banking, nationalize private resources and raise wages. What the platform of his "National Union of Social Justice" finally boiled down to was a sick recipe of isolationism and anti-Semitic invective.

Then there was Dr. Francis E. Townsend of California, who had started a movement based on the proposition that if the federal government gave 200 dollars a month to everybody over sixty who was out of work, provided they spent the money the same month, the nation's ills would be cured overnight. It was amazing how many people went for this idea. I spent a lot of time ridiculing Dr. Townsend and his plan. I called it "another chain letter racket."

Father Coughlin and Dr. Townsend both had some fanatic followers in Ohio. Once a lawyer named Zimmerman threatened me with overwhelming defeat unless I joined up with both of these paragons. When I told Mr. Zimmerman over the phone that the good father ought to get out of politics and stick with his ministry, the lawyer was furious, hinted dark threats against my person and banged down the telephone. Two years later Dr. Townsend, during a Congressional investigation, contempuously refused to answer questions about his use of the mails. That same night the entire Townsend Old Age Organization of seventy-five people, occupying thirteen offices in Washington, cleaned out their files and furniture and silently stole away.

Another phenomenon of the period was Huey Long. He was supposed to represent the poor whites against the planters of Louisiana. He was certainly one of the most colorful figures of the period. He could switch from being a "cracker" to a master politician as the situation demanded. He supported Roosevelt in 1932, but it didn't take him long to start opposing the President. He will probably be remembered better for his studied rudeness and for keeping his hat on in the President's office (he was never invited again) than he will for his questionable achievements. His widow Rose Long, a fine, gentle lady, succeeded him in the Senate following his assassination. His son, Senator Russell Long, is today one of the most respected, effective, studious and hard working members of the United States Senate and well beloved in his state of Louisiana.

As political dictator of Louisiana, Senator Long would stand up in Congress and make endless dramatic speeches. He would do this without notes, which always impressed me.

He frequently came over to the Chamber of the House of Representatives and the Congressmen from his state would gather around him, presumably to take instructions. One Louisiana Representative told me, "Huey Long can make a more intelligent and more eloquent speech when drunk than any other Senator can when sober." I listened admiringly in the Senate Chamber one evening while he was discoursing eloquently in a one-man filibuster that he was undertaking quite successfully. On one occasion at the City Club in Cleveland, he frightened members of our Chamber of Commerce by convincing them they were about to suffer the same fate as the aristocrats in the French Revolution. He sometimes would sit at a prominent table in the Mayflower dining room, a fashionable place in those days, napkin tucked in his collar, spilling food and using his knife and fork in the opposite way from others in the room. Of course he was putting on a show. He was, in fact, a university graduate and an effective governor whose accomplishments for Louisiana endure to this day, though he was ruthless in dealing with political enemies.

Then there was Brigadier General Smedley Butler, who might almost be called the father of the Red Scare tactics in this country. On March 12, 1935, I pointed out that the Communists had polled 102,000 votes in 1932 in the entire country at the low point of the depression and the height of their national popularity, and even fewer votes in 1934. I called

193

Butler "a faker and a publicity hound," whose "fantastical and phantasmagoric tale of Communism in high places among the country's most respected citizens deserved no consideration whatever." I said then, and I still think that public officials or private citizens who seek to suppress freedom of speech are themselves law breakers.

From the radical left came the voice of Upton Sinclair who had distinguished himself not only as a novelist but as a force in helping to get the Pure Food and Drug Act passed in 1906. Now in the thirties he was back with a new and more sweeping cause, an "End Poverty in California" movement. He got a lot of support for it, too, but he was not rewarded with the governorship of the Golden State.

I had my own position clear on the question of propaganda from both far left and far right as early as March 1934. I tried to make a distinction between radicals and conservatives and pleaded that this country should never take action to infringe upon the inherent and fundamental rights of freedom of speech and freedom of the press. I said, "The word *radical* is derived from the Greek word meaning root. A real radical goes to the root of a thing. The most dangerous citizens in this country are not the Communists . . . but the selfish financiers, the big city bankers, who objected strenuously to direct relief for the unemployed, but kept their own hands in the public treasury and took out money for their own selfish uses and purposes.

"The radicals," I said, "have always been the beacon lights of history. They came from the high, they came from the low. Look at the Declaration of Independence and you will see an illustrious roll of radicals on that immortal scroll.

"The greatest radical of all was born in a manger and crucified between two thieves."

If there is anything at all in the Darwinian theory of the origin of the species then perhaps the first monkey who slid down a tree was the first radical. After all, he upset the estab-

194

lished order of things. From the tree tops the conservative monkeys looked down at him and shrieked that he was a lunatic, a radical and a fool. The tail-hold that was good enough for their fathers was good enough for them, but the radical monkey lifted up his head in hope toward heaven, stood erect and walked and in the course of time became a man. The conservatives are still up there looking down. Many radicals in the thirties who strayed to the left were hungry people, unemployed for months on end. Their children were hungry. They yearned for food and shelter. They didn't know what to do. They had lost hope that their government would do anything for them. When people are miserable and helpless and have lost confidence in their leaders, then the Communists prosper, but I don't feel that all the people who turned very briefly toward Communism in the thirties should be haunted by this for the rest of their lives. Take some idealistic girl in the early thirties who couldn't get a job for fifteen dollars a week, and maybe had doubts about our form of government. If she made the mistake of attending a couple of Communist party meetings she could easily have come away with the idea that the answer to all the questions that have plagued mankind since the fall of Adam were on the verge of solution if only she would sign up with this politico-religious crusade. Most party members in those days who stuck around long enough finally caught on to what was really expected—a surrender of the people's rights in the name of just one more brand of dictatorship. But that girl should not be penalized thirty years later because she was misled then.

In August 1935, my colleague and running mate, Charles V. Truax, a hardy and robust man, died suddenly of a heart attack. The very first speech he had made in the House of Representatives was in behalf of the farmers. The last speech he had ever made had been on the same subject. He had been a conscientious Congressman, cheerful and industrious,

195

if something of a rabble rouser. As an orator he would out-do most present-day Senators. He wore himself out serving his constituency and the country. We had disagreed on a number of political issues, but his death was a terrible blow to me.

During my second term as a Congressman I voted in favor of social security, regulation of holding companies, a minority bill never passed to establish a farm credit system, and against bonuses for veterans.

I opposed the administration's act authorizing the Secretary of Agriculture to make benefit payments up to five million dollars to farmers who would take land out of production for soil conservation purposes. This struck me as a topsy-turvy approach to conservation and farm production problems. And when Roosevelt began to pack the Supreme Court to prevent having his recovery legislation barred as unconstitutional, I did not find it in my heart to cheer him on, even though I defended the moves he made in public speeches and called the fight between Roosevelt and the Court "the struggle between those who look forward with hope into the future and those reactionaries who tolerate the past and dread the future." Yet it is certainly true that many supporters of the "Nine Old Men" had motives less pure than they professed. Lawyers opposing Roosevelt said if recovery laws were contrary to the letter of the Constitution, then a Constitutional amendment should be referred to the people. I know I wasn't all wrong when I remarked at this that "if you want to know what the people don't think, get the *Literary Digest* to take another poll." But in looking at that period in perspective I think President Roosevelt did try to go too far with regard to the High Court.

In his first term in office as our Chief Executive, Franklin Roosevelt actually led an American revolution. It differed from other revolutions because, instead of destroying lives, it saved lives. It overturned the existing order. Life in America was not the same after the Roosevelt revolution and it will never be the same again. Roosevelt's Republican opponent in 1936 said he was regimenting the American people, that people would have to wear dog tags, that the Social Security Act was the worst thing that ever happened in this country. The Republican platform preached repeal of the Social Security Act and though the G. O. P. Presidential candidate was Governor Alf Landon of Kansas, a highly respected and competent candidate, he lost all but two states. The Roosevelt revolution was accomplished not only without bloodshed, but without abrogating one iota of the civil rights of this country's citizens. The detractors of Roosevelt will tell you he tried to crush free enterprise, but actually he accelerated and strengthened the free enterprise system. He made it tenable for capitalism to survive. That is why I supported him.

When I came back to Cleveland the bread lines and soup kitchens of the earlier era had already disappeared. New stores were going up. The city looked different. People were more alive and better dressed. They looked happier and more prosperous. The feeling of recovery was in the air. Wherever you looked you could see the evidence.

But I was not to return just yet to my seat in Congress.

What kept me out of Congress in 1936 was a try for the Democratic nomination for Governor of Ohio. The incumbent was Governor Martin L. Davey. He had no love for me and, in fact, put up another candidate in addition to himself to weaken my chances.

Political contributions to my candidacy were few. Mostly I spent whatever money of my own I managed to scrape up. Headquarters were in my law office and there were no funds to open branches in Columbus, Akron or other Ohio cities. I came out openly against the state 3 percent sales tax, especially as it applied to groceries, medicines and other necessities, and spoke repeatedly against sales and excise taxes because they were not levied according to ability to pay. This position did not make me popular with Chamber of Commerce circles and the big businessmen who helped grease the wheels of the state political machines. I had braved the opposition of Governor Davey because Harry Hopkins and other administration leaders in Washington had urged me to abandon an almost certain race for re-election as Congressman-at-large to campaign for governor. They had promised to help, but no help came through. I did pile up some votes against Governor Davey, which surprised his supporters among the Democratic county chairmen. I came in second, but in politics second is as good as last. (In retrospect I wonder why I ever wanted to be Governor.)

I made no effort to secure an appointive position under federal authority. Instead, Ruby and I set up housekeeping in Cleveland Heights once more. Soon I was practising law again as a private citizen.

My work was as a trial lawyer, which meant I was trying law suits for the most part on behalf of other lawyers who did not go into the courtroom. I defended many criminal cases in the Ohio courts and in the United States District Court for the Northern District of Ohio.

Despite the pressure of work those were good years for Ruby and me. I began to forget about Washington—the lobbyists, the pressure groups, piles of mail, the days with no time for lunch. It had felt good to be taking part in the making of legislation that had helped millions of idle people to find work and millions of hungry people to eat again, but it also felt good to walk into court with a clear-cut case, to be arguing the law again instead of helping to manufacture it. After the hectic pace of Washington, life in Cleveland seemed relatively unhurried, more dignified and more human. We saw our old friends again and got to know our own family, who in turn learned more about us including the fact that one of my real weaknessess is a set of private superstitions.

I always go around the outside of ladders, if only to be on the safe side. I never put my hat on a bed or open an umbrella in a house. I am a pushover for fortune tellers. I remember one time shortly after our marriage Ruby went to see a certain Madame Gudekuntz, who had established a reputation in Cleveland as a seer. She didn't even need cards or a crystal ball to tell you how things were going to come out. She would just look at you. She told my wife she would die before I did. But she saw me swinging something like a racquet and said that I would probably die doing something athletic. Ruby promptly tried to keep me away from the tennis court. She also told my wife I was going to be Governor of Ohio. She didn't say anything about an astronaut in my life, but on the whole I would say she had me well pegged.

The purpose of the legal profession is for citizens always to have at their disposal trained men to protect them, men who will stand up before arbitrary power from whatever quarter and assert the inalienable rights of the individual to his freedoms. A good trial lawyer is more than a man of law; he should be a man of letters. Above all, he should be a man with a decent regard for the feelings of other men. The counsel for the accused in a criminal case has a solemn responsibility. The right of an accused to confide in his counsel without fear of disclosure is regarded as so sacred that it stands among the most firmly established principles in our law. Under our Constitution a person accused of a crime not only *may* be heard, but *must* be heard. The lawyer who defends him is invested with high privileges for the benefit of the defendant. He speaks not only for the individual who has been charged with the crime, but for all defendants who may at any time find themselves in like circumstances. I did

199

not regard as second-rate or small-time the job I was doing as a defense lawyer in Cleveland.

And yet, when the opportunity came again in 1938 to run for Congress, I could not resist it. I made a hard race for the Democratic nomination for Congressman-at-large. Once again I was a runner with no organization, no political machine to assure victory by, as it were, political automation. Ohio Congressmen-at-large at the time were Harold Mosier and John McSweeney. Mosier, who had been Lieutenant-Governor of the state, was running for a second term. Once, when I was campaigning for the nomination, Governor Davey, who had never tired of disliking me, tried to deny me the platform because he knew I was going to denounce Congressman Mosier, who had become an opponent of President Roosevelt's policies. The Governor said he was paying for the hall and the meeting arrangements and he didn't want "personalities" injected into the speeches. I did not defer to his wishes, but as a general rule I gave up attending meetings arranged by Davey's organization. I traveled around the state making speeches wherever I could find an audience of six or more Democrats.

On primary night I learned that I had won a considerable victory, running first in a field of three. John McSweeney, who had served a number of terms in Congress, came in second. Mosier limped in third. Governor Davey lost his bid for the Democratic nomination for a third term as Governor to Charles Sawyer of Cincinnati, who later served as Secretary of Commerce in Harry Truman's cabinet.

After that the party in Ohio was torn asunder by a feud between the two men. According to Davey, Sawyer never had the courtesy to acknowledge the congratulatory message he received from the defeated Governor. I don't know whether this was true or not, but I do know that both Congressman McSweeney and myself spoke to Sawyer, urging him to call on the Governor and try to make peace with him.

200

There was no peace, however. My running mate, Mc-Sweeney, and I became the real victims of this feud. My Republican opponent, George H. Bender, who had been defeated in 1934 and 1936, defeated John McSweeney; the other Republican candidate, L. L. Marshall, a Cleveland lawyer, defeated me. At that time names did not rotate on the Ohio ballot but were printed in alphabetical order, which gave a distinct advantage to the top candidate for an office for which two or more were to be elected.

For months I had neglected my law business. Driving long distances by car, I didn't get back to my home in Cleveland Heights until two or three in the morning. Ruby had been with me on all those trips and she never complained. In fact as we frequently drove until two or three in the morning, she figured her principal duty was to talk to me and keep me awake. I appreciate now how difficult this campaigning must have been for her but frankly I enjoyed it.

I had spent a lot of money on the Congressional campaign and my neglected law business was yielding poor earnings. The only ray of sunshine that lighted the gloom was my daughter's marriage to Robert R. Richardson of Cleveland Heights in November 1938, shortly after the election.

I began to concentrate intensely on my practice. Ruby and I could live comfortably again. We took several vacation trips through Canada. Life was pleasant and free of hardship, yet when the clarion call of politics sounded again in 1940 I listened and obeyed.

In 1940 for the last time Ohio was to elect two Congressmen-at-large. There was a contest for the Democratic nominations. Francis Durbin of Lima, son of William Durbin who had been state chairman, won one of the nominations and I the other. Our Republican opponents were the incumbents, George H. Bender and L. L. Marshall, both seeking second terms. Francis Durbin was a typical ward politician who had gone up the ladder. He never overlooked an

201

opportunity to make a speech; even at the 1940 Democratic National Convention, he sounded off to the delegates although not on the program as a speaker. He campaigned vigorously. So did I. When Roosevelt came to Ohio seeking votes for his own renomination, I visited him on his Presidential train and accompanied him to several cities. I worked harder than I ever had before. The traveling, the speechmaking, even the additional responsibility of trying at the same time to keep my law business active and solvent, seemed to agree with me. I had no state-wide organization and the going was difficult, but nothing downed my spirits.

Bender defeated Durbin, but I defeated Marshall. In a year when a majority of the Ohio legislators elected were Republicans, I had run ahead of most of my ticket.

Ruby and I rented a large apartment on Kalorama Road near the Shoreham Hotel in the northwest section of Washington. The city was different from what it had been in 1933. Roosevelt was a familiar figure whose supporters no longer stood in awe of him and whose enemies felt free to speak out ever more loudly against his tactics and policies. The city did not seem to hang, as it had, on an emotional cliff edge of anxious expectancy. Nor was there that sense of united purpose which a crisis brings.

Although I had lost seniority, my former colleagues welcomed me with great warmth. Warren Magnuson and John McCormick were particularly cordial. They pushed me ahead quite a bit in the Seventy-seventh Congress. Yet I was, politically, at a low ebb. I had opposed the Townsend Plan and the Townsendites still hated me. My reputation as a "loner" on the political scene made many politicians wary of me. I began to reconsider some of my uncompromising methods. The mature politician may be totally uncorrupt but, at the same time, he must, through the years, have

202

learned that you cannot argue about everything, that you cannot fight everyone at once, that you cannot remake the world overnight. In a democracy, lawmaking is largely a matter of compromise. If you want to accomplish anything in committee, you have to get used to giving a little on one point to gain elsewhere. It takes time to learn these lessons.

Ruby and I felt much more at home in the capital than we had in former years. We still didn't entertain much, but we had many friends. I played tennis, whenever there was time from Congressional duties, with Henry Wallace. Frequently in the club locker room I had friendly conversations with Supreme Court Justice Hugo Black, who was and is an excellent tennis player. Another frequent opponent at tennis was Mom Luang Kharb Kunjara, military attaché of the Embassy of Thailand who had been educated at Oxford. We struck up a friendship at the Army-Navy Country Club and pretty soon I guess I was on friendly terms with just about everybody connected with the Thai Embassy. There was a tremendous amount of hard work connected with being Congressman-at-large from a state as populous as Ohio, but Ruby and I were happy.

One of the speeches I am glad I made in Congress in 1941 was a salute to Secretary of State Cordell Hull. I predicted that the Good Neighbor Policy, which he played so large a part in bringing about, would be recorded as his greatest achievement.

It was getting harder and harder to ignore the rest of the world. The war I had classified as a less grim prospect than unemployment was now a reality and was coming close. In Ohio cities like Ashtabula, Lorain and Cleveland, war vessels were under construction.

Soon Pearl Harbor, which American high-ranking naval officers had assured us was impregnable, was the scene of our greatest naval defeat. Once again the scattered forces of Congress rallied behind Roosevelt. Those who had refused to go along with the administration in extending the tours of duty of men already drafted under the Selective Service Act and recalling retired Army personnel, now atoned for the lack of attention the United States had paid to the rest of the world during the depression years. We did nothing to block the acceleration of the war machinery needed to turn the nation that had experienced the black Sunday of Pearl Harbor into a country geared for victory.

Europe had always seemed far away, even in the prewar years when the German-American Bund was holding picnics and marching in my own state of Ohio. Most of us had believed that Chamberlain would take care of Hitler, and anyone who denies that now is simply rewriting his personal history to accord with the requirements of public relations. Although I was one of the first to denounce Hitler on the floor of Congress, I never believed he would overrun Europe. But shortly before Pearl Harbor many of us became afraid. If we had known of the plans already on the books in Japan and Germany to bomb New York and our great industrial centers, and systematically reduce America to the state of slavery, we might have been even more frightened. Only a few months earlier I had been saying, "The National Defense bill, for which I intend to vote, does not change our status as a non-belligerent. Nor is it a device to get us into war without consent of Congress . . . nor does it involve the surrender of our war-making powers to one man. We are not at war. In my judgment this is not a war Congress . . ."

How academic all that was now! By May 1942, the Seventy-seventh Congress, awake at last to the conflagration that threatened to consume the world, hastily backed pay increases for service men, supported military appropriations totalling 43 billion dollars—more than our government had spent altogether between 1789 and 1918—provided for drafting men of eighteen and nineteen. After three terms as Con-

204

gressman-at-large, I went home to Ohio to run for re-election in November of 1942.

I said in one speech, "This office belongs to the sovereign people of Ohio. It does not belong to me . . ." I turned out to be right in a sense I never intended. *Time* magazine had called me the "best Democratic vote-getter in Ohio" shortly before, but a reapportionment due to the 1940 census entitled my state to one Congressman-at-large instead of two, as before. *Time's* encomium didn't help. But, as it happened, I had already taken steps to join the Army. When George Bender defeated me again, I decided it was time to vote for a personal selective service act that would put his country's uniform on Stephen M. Young.

CHAPTER 15

✄ *It turned out to be harder to get into the war than into Congress. All I wanted was a commission in some branch of our armed forces. I tried through Admiral Nimitz to join the Navy. As a Congressman, I had helped to get a young man named James Hunter Drum into West Point and I went to New York to see his father, General Hugh Drum, to offer my services to the Army. At last, after a number of other interviews General Drum had managed to arrange, I was ordered to active duty as a major.*

I already had one son, Stephen Junior, in the navy. He had enlisted the day after Pearl Harbor, and I had been proud to see his picture in the Cleveland *Press.* Then, in September 1942, my younger boy, Richard, a sophomore at the University of North Carolina, telephoned from Chapel Hill to ask if he also could join the Navy. Ruby was pretty unhappy—Dick was still a minor—but she didn't hold him back. We signed permission for him to enlist.

Meanwhile, Ruby and I had closed our apartment in Washington. She went home to Cleveland and I went to the University of Virginia for three months' preparation for the life of an Army officer. At the age of fifty-two it certainly felt strange to be back in school, listening to lectures, taking notes, learning German, French and Italian, boning up on the subject of military government—information that was to prove more valuable in a few years than I ever dreamed.

Particularly uncomfortable for anyone accustomed to the sedentary life of Congress, where you only get up on your feet to make a speech, was the business of drilling. I shudder to remember it. Later I was detailed to Camp Custer and went out into the field for basic training, and I don't like to remember that, either.

But in Charlottesville there were all the comforts of home. I had a room in the luxurious home of Mrs. Twyman, whose husband had been mayor. For thirty dollars a month those were fine quarters. I had a big bedroom, a dressing room and one luxury I will never forget, a pink private bath. The entertainment at Mrs. Twyman's was home-grown; she and her sister and their friends would get together and sing.

After a shower in my pink bathroom I would go out early every morning to face the military life. I had all my meals in a cafeteria near the Law School of the University of Virginia. Then I would rush off doubletime to early classes. Everything was always doubletime.

Life in Camp Custer, where I was ordered in July 1943, was quite a contrast. Instead of Mrs. Twyman's homey bedroom, there was a barracks with one hundred and fifty soldiers, military government people and enlisted men. You were always either running or waiting—to shave, to eat, to receive instructions. The smartest fellow I saw at Camp Custer was a Negro captain from Cleveland. He would get up at 4:00 every morning so that he could wash and shave and get dressed in peace.

I found it easy to get a thumb caught in my M-1 rifle. It took me a while to learn to make up my bunk properly. Later in the month I got the news that Dick was on his way overseas, and I worried about him.

Soon afterwards I finally was alerted for overseas duty, and reported to the staging area at Fort Myers. There I was placed in command of an officers' detachment. It was easy to write in my diary: "War is a terrible thing; war is the su-

208

preme enemy of mankind." Fine words, but I didn't know then what they really meant. The only "hardships" I encountered at Fort Myers were numerous bedbug bites. In fact, this particular barrack was so infested (or else they joined in assailing me) that I took to the luxury of staying in a Washington hotel and reporting back at six in the morning.

We left in the middle of August for Newport News, Virginia, and the staging area at Camp Patrick Henry. The camp was in a frenzied state of disorganization, but in our enthusiasm and the hope of going overseas shortly, all of us took dirt, discomfort, disorder, poor food and inadequate sanitation in our stride. After one false alert to proceed to a port of embarkation we finally left the barracks of Camp Henry on August 25th on a steaming hot day. I was carrying a full pack, steel helmet, blanket roll, gas mask, .45 automatic and a canteen filled with water. At Hampton Roads we boarded a ferry for a steamer that would take us to North Africa.

The *Del Norte* was one of a convoy of eighty-two vessels. Our captain wanted to bet me two dollars our first night out that we would be attacked before we reached Algiers. One evening in September an armed freighter just ahead of us fired on a submarine. The following evening another sub was detected just off our forward bow. A destroyer dropped six depth charges and sank the sub.

Our journey to North Africa took twenty-two days. At last, on September 18th, we anchored in the Bay of Bizerte. Although Bizerte was a ghost city—only the outer walls were left of many buildings—the white, pink and blue stucco buildings which still stood were beautiful. There remains in my mind the vivid image of a Catholic church with a statue of the Saviour undamaged and looking down on the scene like an omen of hope.

My first night in North Africa was spent on a hill over Bizerte. I bivouacked under an olive tree, sleeping on the ground about ten feet from a large latrine. The only enemies I fought were mosquitoes and flies. Before the night was over I bade them farewell, but they knew better. We packed and left camp about 2 a. m. on a cold morning in trucks for a relay stage where we boarded an old French train for Algiers. The trip took four days.

The flies and mosquitoes and bugs had boarded with us. They made sleep almost impossible. From the window I looked out at wrecked German tanks and thousands of other wrecked and captured Axis vehicles. We passed towns where the natives lived as they had for two thousand years. The temperature was always above 100 degrees. There was no running water on the train. The temperature rose to 112. In mid-afternoon and again at sunset we would stop to prepare our meals. We would sit beside the tracks eating our rations and boiling our coffee with water obtained locally. At last we arrived in the dazzling white city of Algiers. From Algiers we were taken by truck to a place called Tizi-Ouzou some forty miles away. This turned out to be a pretty dirty city, as I learned when I took a walk downtown that first day.

In Tizi-Ouzou the days were hot and the nights were cold. We arrived just in time for the rainy season. The water flooded our floorless tents. There was a school of military government where we continued our Italian lessons. There were no cables or letters from home for me.

I bunked with several other American officers in a tent. Nearby in another tent there were English officers. It happened that one of our men, because of a broken nose he had sustained in his college days, was a loud snorer. The first night there, shortly after the snoring reached full volume around three in the morning, an English lieutenant poked his flashlight into our tent, probing for the culprit.

"By God, man," he roared indignantly, "You're making a

bloody awful noise with that snoring. Cease and desist." Together we prompted this insufferable ally to beat a hasty retreat and that was the beginning of a private war-within-a-war which I found myself carrying on against the English. But soon I was to see real injustice which reduced such incidents to microscopic proportions.

The war showed me I had never known what real injustice was. The hardships I had talked about on the floor of Congress—hunger, unemployment, homelessness, poverty—were things I knew about mainly through hearsay. But I remember going into a house in a town in North Africa with little shelves cut into the sides of the walls for the family to sleep on. I had to revise my ideas of what a house was, what a home was. This was only the beginning. Out of it all I learned this much: war makes men bigger than they are and smaller than they are. Some are impelled to acts more than human. Others are driven to behavior less than human. I saw more humanity and more inhumanity in my few years overseas in wartime than I might have witnessed in a lifetime had I stayed home. I learned the meanings of the words in my own speeches. I would never be able to say them glibly again—hunger, homelessness, poverty.

In the middle of October, along with four other majors commanding the platoon, I left Algiers. We boarded a Liberty ship for Italy. The next morning we learned that Italy had declared war on Germany.

Later in October we lifted anchor at Malta and headed northwest for Naples. We passed through the Strait of Messina where Ulysses was tied to the mast so that he wouldn't be lured by the sound of the Sirens. We saw no Sirens, only some of our "co-belligerents" in rowboats, begging for cigarettes.

We arrived in Naples in the midst of a blackout. The enemy still had air superiority in 1943 and all of Italy and North Africa was blacked out nightly. I wondered if my son were somewhere in the same dark city. On the first of November the Germans raided in force—just one month after our troops had captured the city. I saw a bomb smash an apartment and kill some soldiers and a little child. The Germans raided the city every night.

The filth of Naples was appalling. The water supply had been cut off. There were lines of people going to pumps for water. People lay down in the street because they weren't strong enough to walk. Shortly after arriving in Naples I was ordered to take charge in the town of Nola, which is part of the province of Naples, and about twenty miles from the city.

On the road to Nola our jeep broke down. Tanks and tired men were going along the road in a steady stream. We found ourselves near a village called Marigliano, a miserable, hostile, uninviting-looking place with cheap shops and walled-in homes close to the road. It was cold and raining hard. An English sergeant was standing close to our jeep. He didn't seem to notice us, he was looking across the street. Without so much as turning his head he said, "Funny how kids all hold their dolls the same way."

I looked across the narrow road. A few yards away I saw a little girl, barefoot and thin, in a doorway. She was gazing balefully in our direction and at the rain, stepping back a little every time a tank or a truck or a motor vehicle went by throwing mud and water in her direction. With one arm she clutched a baby doll. Its head was level with her neck. How firmly she clasped the doll's arm with her little hand! She was trying hard to keep her doll secure against any threat. The sergeant walked away. I thought of my three-year-old grand-daughter, Gail, and then wrote to her about the little girl and the doll. I wrote that it seemed to me the Italian child was symbolic of children everywhere, clinging to their dolls and stepping back as the vehicles of hatred and cruelty and oppression and war rattled past. My letter found its way into the newspapers of Cleveland, along with a pic-

212

ture of little Gail looking extremely uncomfortable about the whole thing.

There was no electricity in Nola. About a week after I got there I had to act as a summary court and sentence a woman for black market operations. I suspended the sentence after she had served a half day in jail. She had already been in prison for eight days waiting for a decision on her case.

Once I went for a walk and a little boy ran out and kissed my hand. I was deeply embarrassed. But I also remember hungry women who surrounded me, screaming, gesticulating, showing me pieces of some poor quality bread. One spat in my face. I tried to tell them it was not my fault that the bread was poor and scarce, that their little king had declared war on our nation, that a short while ago they themselves had been shouting *"Duce, Duce, Duce,"* that I was only there to maintain law and order. I had to deal with people I probably would never have met in the normal course of events—black marketeers who were rumored to have been members of Dutch Schultz's mob in New York, madams from the local brothels, demonstrators, more women and children gesticulating outside my office in the public square. All around us the war raged—bombings, artillery battles, shellings. And it rained almost constantly.

At last, shortly before Christmas, I left Nola. I had tried to do a few things—tripling the food allowance for prisoners, trying to improve the town's food, trying to reassure the frightened and despairing people. Christmas found me back in Naples. I learned that my son Stephen had been injured in combat in the Pacific. On Christmas Eve the German airplanes came over in force and the explosion of bombs and anti-aircraft fire lighted up Naples. It was a beautiful and fearsome sight. My most vivid memory of Christmas Day, 1943, was of a barefoot man lying unconscious in the business section of Naples. An Italian *carabiniere* paid him no heed. An American soldier and I tried to help him but he

213

seemed to be starving and beyond help. Since there was no hospital in town we had him moved to the local prison where we learned that he was suffering from severe malnutrition. Later it was reported that he had died. In the evening the orchestra at the small hotel where some of us were staying played "White Christmas," "Margie" and "Lili Marlene."

The Germans helped Naples celebrate the new year with an air raid. The winter became bitter cold. I wore a long-sleeved undershirt, long heavy underdrawers for the first time I can remember, a sweater-vest, a wool shirt and a field jacket, and on top of that my overcoat. Even so, I was always cold. I had trouble with my right foot. There had been some injury to the arch when I had been in accidental contact with a fast-moving jeep, and it bothered me for a long time. I limped around like an old man.

In February I witnessed an incident that to me is the very essence of the ugliness and futility of warfare. An American captain named McIntire was standing outside an area fenced off with barbed wire until it could be cleared of German land mines. A little girl was leaning against the fence crying bitterly. Her pet, a grimy little dog desperately in need of a bath, had wandered into the mine field and detonated one of the anti-personnel mines. The dog was badly injured and whimpering. Captain McIntire went out and tried to comfort the child. It seemed she was going to cry as long as her pet lay helplessly in pain. McIntire didn't want to shoot the dog with its little mistress standing there. He stepped across the barbed wire. Soon he had the dog in his arms and was starting back toward the girl. She stood there looking up at him with her eyes shining with gratitude through her tears, waiting at the wire fence for her dog. McIntire's attention was diverted for a split second and he stepped on a hidden mine. He and the injured dog were killed at once. I don't know what happened to the little girl. I wonder if she is still alive.

I wonder if she remembers that a soldier from a distant land lost his life because a dog whimpered and a child cried.

In February I was up at the Anzio-Nettuno beachhead. A few other officers, enlisted men and myself were sleeping in a subbasement, an old wine cellar perhaps thirty feet underground. We slept on bed springs or anything we could scrounge from partly destroyed houses nearby, constantly aware that a direct hit from artillery or a bomb would take care of us, but good. The Germans were shelling us at least once every hour. I remember that I was about to fall asleep one night when a rat ran across my mouth. The Germans were steadily bombing Anzio and Nettuno Harbor from the surrounding heights. It seemed for a time that we were like cockroaches in a bath tub. The cold and the rain continued.

There were days when one air raid followed another. We were living on C and K rations. Under a pelting rain we lived through the loading of scores of civilian refugees who were to be taken by LST boats to Naples. In the days that followed I learned about foxholes. Once I spent hours talking to three GI's in a foxhole while the German bombs smashed all around us. Soon afterwards the American bombers came over. I had never expected to see my wet, chilly, rat-and-lice infested wine cellar ever again, much less to love it, but how glad I was to get back there that night. A few days later at the cemetery I saw German and American dead placed in mattress covers and buried. There were two German soldiers who had been killed while their hands gripped a barbed wire fence. The wire had to be clipped with wire cutters close to their hands. They were very young. They had never even shaved. Poor little supermen!

In my wine cellar there were electric lights now and the dubious comfort of the notorious Axis Sally, an American turned German propagandist, who used to play happy music from Berlin and assure her American listeners of a glamorous life if they would only surrender. In March the air raids and the heavy fighting continued. I met Ernie Pyle, the war correspondent, and we played cards as Axis Sally entertained us by radio, telling us, "Easy, boys, there is danger ahead," and singing "Lili Marlene" most alluringly. I had grown to like that song so much I was working on my own English translation of it. A lot of us were beginning to rely more and more on this woman for entertainment. I will never forget her broadcast of "My Old Kentucky Home" sandwiched in between lists of war prisoners. After giving the names and serial numbers of some captured American soldiers, Axis Sally would always say happily, "For them the war is over. They will be returned safely to their homes and loved ones. Easy, boys. There's danger ahead."

While I was at Anzio a letter from my brother Henry told me that my sister Wally had died on January 14th. I felt more desolate than I ever had in my life—and I couldn't shed a tear. Perhaps I had seen too much horror and destruction, too much of death.

Late in March the commanding major general of the Sixth Corps of the Fifth Army ordered a number of us officers back to Naples. On June 5, 1944, I entered downtown Rome where I had been sent on a temporary assignment. I have never seen such demonstrations of hysterical joy. Throngs of Romans surrounded our jeeps. Women and children kissed our hands. Flowers were thrown at us. People were laughing and crying, shouting and dancing in the streets. I remember a girl about eighteen weeping and laughing all at once and crying out over and over, "Why did you take so long?"

Our engineers were trying to bring water and electricity into the great city. I had to direct the burial of a dead German soldier and a couple of Italian Fascists killed by "patriots." These Fascist civilians, many of whom allegedly shot our soldiers in the back, were buried without ceremony, not even a prayer. I directed that the dead soldier and others I had buried later be given honors and prayer from a member of the clergy or an American chaplain, if one could be found. On June 6th we learned that Allied troops had landed in France. The war was going well. In February I had been lying in the mud of Sisterna de Lattoria while machine-guns strafed the ground and shells burst and flares lit up the sky. Now in June I drove into Sisterna de Lattoria. The city was a mass of rubble. A beautiful cathedral had been leveled to the ground.

Early in July I sat as one of three judges in a general military court, trying a man named Carlo Barghiliogni and a woman named Olga Spera, both accused of spying for the Germans. They had been sent across the line near Minturno by the Germans to report back what they could learn. He was a fifty-nine-year-old former army captain and she was a school teacher of forty-eight. Major Henry Glenn, a Fifth Army officer who had been in a New York law firm, was the prosecutor. Judge Robert Woodward of Chicago defended.

My associates on the bench were Major Paul Shriver, a former federal official from Colorado who was then head of the Rome Allied Property Control Office, and Lieutenant Colonel John Willis, an English barrister attached to the legal division of the Rome Allied Area Command. Lieutenant Colonel Willis presided.

The woman was frightened and ugly—far from the Mata Hari one might have hoped for—and the man looked more than his middle age. They had been sent by the Germans to pose as a refugee couple trying to get back to their home in southern Italy. Meanwhile, they were supposed to take notice of the sleeve patches of Allied soldiers and troop concentrations. They claimed they had had a change of heart, but they had been well paid for their services and when they were seized in Minturno, a town held by the Allies, they had

217

confessed quickly. As spies they were entitled to a fair trial under the Hague Convention's international rules of warfare. A few days later, by majority vote, the court rendered its verdict of guilty, with a twenty-year sentence for Barghiliogni and eighteen for Spera. I did not concur. I voted for the death penalty by shooting for the man, and life imprisonment for the woman.

An important witness was an American captain, a counterintelligence officer. The entire case was written up for the *New Yorker* by Daniel Lang, who was present at the trial. He gave the American captain the name of Costello in his report to protect his identity. At the end of his article Mr. Lang wrote:

"The MP's led the prisoners off. Barghiliogni had a rather sullen look on his face, but the woman was lively. She wanted to walk faster than her guard. Major Woodward was picking up his papers and Major Shriver from the bench arranged to meet him and Major Young outside the palace for a lift. Then Captain Costello came up alongside me as I was leaving the courtroom. He was blearyeyed. 'Holy Mackerel!' he said as we went down the corridor. 'If I had known it was going to be this much trouble for the U. S. Army, I might have let those two get away.'"

I, on the other hand, was surprised at the light sentence dealt out by my colleagues. At the same time, I was surprised at my surprise, wondering whether the war had changed me, made me that hard. Yet during the months of warfare my principal companion had been a cold in the head. My foot continued to bother me even though the medics had pronounced it healed. My injured ankle remained swollen and stiff.

I went back to Nettuno during the summer of 1944. Both Nettuno and Anzio were broken, ruined cities. The odor of flowers was strong, but the stench of death was stronger. One does not forget the smell of powder in battle, or the sickening sweet smell of the dead.

In August I was assigned to the Palace of Justice in Rome to try criminal cases as one of the judges of the summary military court while the Eighth Army fought on the outskirts of Florence. I passed judgment on seventy-four criminal cases in a single day, until the Italian clerks and the prosecutor begged me to quit long enough for them to catch up with the clerical work. A few days later I reduced the number of cases tried to fifty.

On August 14th I left Rome for Orvieto in a truck. Orvieto is a beautiful little medieval town on top of a hill surrounded by a wall. I was not sorry to leave Rome. I felt that when I was in the field like this I was in the war. And I saw a cruel spectacle. A yelling crowd paraded a young fellow and a young woman up and down the main street. The young woman's hair was clipped in front across the top. Presumably, they were Fascists.

Although I was assigned to the Fifth Army, now I was actually serving in the Eighth Army. We were preparing to go into the province of Reggio. We passed through the most beautiful towns of Tuscany. Wherever we went were ruined churches, damaged frescoes. In Florence I was supposed to assist in the administration of the city. There was fighting in the streets. It was boiling hot. The Germans were shelling the city. I was put in charge of handling all refugees in the Fifth Army area. I drove out with a Red Cross official to within seven hundred and fifty yards of the German lines. The refugees came through the sewers and were brought up on ladders out of manholes. All the men in one group of thirty-two required hospitalization. I saw one woman carrying a wounded man on her back.

By early September we had driven the Germans out of Florence, although some of them returned at night on patrol or possibly to see their Italian girl friends, and there were nuisance raids. They had killed three hundred civilians and wounded one thousand, three hundred and eight Florentines, and, of course, some Americans.

In October there were food lines in the city and in that month I received in the mail a memorable and morale-lifting envelope: it contained two *Congressional Records*. I still had my cold.

In November we read of President Roosevelt's re-election. I was overjoyed.

When the work of the refugee division was over, I became chief of the economics and supply division. Later I was sent to Montecatini Terme in central Italy as civil affairs officer, and later as Allied military governor of the entire province. Montecatini Terme is a beautiful health resort famous for its baths; when I took one of them, my war-long cold, which had at last cleared up, promptly returned. By this time I had administered thirty-eight communes in various parts of Italy, many of them in large cities. My son Dick had been in the Solomon Islands campaign, in the invasion of New Guinea, in the Marianas and the Philippines, mostly under heavy enemy fire according to letters I received. Stephen Junior was in a Navy hospital somewhere. One day in Montecatini Terme I arrested a man who was selling bad brandy in old bottles to soldiers. My sentence was to make him drink the bottle he had left instead of selling it for 900 lira. I understand he survived. On Christmas Eve it snowed. My nose was completely blocked from a cold. "To hell with sunny Italy," I told anybody who would listen. "If I ever decide to retire I'll pick a sunny place in the U. S. . . ."

The Red Cross wanted a building in Montecatini Terme which was occupied by a young *signorina*. The secretary of the commune found another apartment for her, but it was not to her liking. After the *carabinieri* moved her furniture into the yard she gave up. One chap in my outfit told her,

"*Il Governatore* is a hard man, the kind who burns orphanages, throws women's furniture into the street and kicks them in the face." But when the secretary of the commune learned I had called the local druggists and blasted them for purchasing hair oil, perfume, knickknacks, and odds and ends instead of medicine, he said, "I hope *Il Governatore* will be running Montecatini a long time!" One of my most satisfactory accomplishments was to end a two-man crime wave in the town; two American soldiers, one a deserter, had been the culprits.

I was having breakfast in the small hotel in Montecatini Terme where I lodged when I received word that President Franklin D. Roosevelt had died. A major from North Carolina telephoned his tragic information. He asked me if I would make the announcement to his soldiers who were bivouacked in a nearby field. He said he could not bear to do it. I went over to the field that was used for religious services. I said, "Soldiers," and then I had to stop for a minute. I said, "I have a sad announcement to make. The President of the United States died at Warm Springs, Georgia. Harry S. Truman is now President of the United States. The war will go on." Many of the soldiers wept. So did I.

Soon afterwards German resistance collapsed. On May 7th Germany surrendered unconditionally. I applied for service in Japan where the war was still raging. I was motivated, I think, by my hope that if accepted I would be given thirty days in Cleveland to be with my wife whom I had not seen for so long. This application was pending when in August President Truman ordered the first atomic bombs dropped on Hiroshima and Nagasaki. We had destroyed the Japanese navy, yet they were planning a direct invasion which might have cost 500,000 lives. Hindsight always provides the best strategy and perhaps we could have prevailed with conventional bombings, but at the time I thought Truman was right to use the bomb. There didn't seem to be any alternative. Russia declared war on Japan and invaded Manchuria. Japan surrendered unconditionally August 14th. The fighting was over, but I was not to see America again just yet. I was to stay on as Allied military governor of Reggio nell' Emilia for many months more.

The Allied military government helped Italy overcome the chaos that might have followed in the wake of the fighting. It laid the foundations on which a free Italy could again become a responsible nation. Allied military government marked a new departure in the ways of men. Never before in history had a conquering army permitted the occupied territory to have a voice in its own management while war was still in progress. The task was complicated by the ruin the Germans had left behind and by the disease of lingering Fascist groups. Twenty years under Mussolini had corroded the Italians' sense of responsibility. Already demagogues were screaming for personal power and aggrandizement at public expense.

In trying to administer communes in Italy I had learned about municipal administration the hard way. Imagine what it would be like to be mayor of a city in Ohio if all the food had been taken away, if women and children had been killed and injured, if there were unburied dead in the streets, if the electric light plant and the gas works had been destroyed, if public services and factories had been ruined, if homes had been demolished, if jails had been broken into and prisoners lynched, if there were thousands of homeless refugees and the people had lost faith in themselves and their government. That was the situation in Italy after the war. We distributed food, maintained order and tried to establish justice. We tried to teach that liberty does not mean license, that freedom does not mean anarchy. All this added up to a daring, intelligent and difficult experiment in democracy.

It seemed to me that any problems I might face at home would be easy by comparison.

222

CHAPTER 16

🦋 *When the war with Japan was over in mid-August, I had
no more duties to perform. They "redeployed" me. I sweated
it out in Rome until November 4th. While I waited I sent a
money order to my son Dick as a wedding present. I sent a
cigarette case and an Imperator Augustus pin to Ruby.*

At last I left by truck for Naples and a week later was on
board the steamer *Santa Barbara* in command of three officers and one hundred and twenty-four enlisted men. The big
thrill of the trip was getting real milk and fresh bread and
eggs and bacon. I have a vivid memory of a steak dinner on
November 20th and a long sleep in the barracks in Pennsylvania. I had never thought of myself as a soldier; I was a
civilian in uniform, but I highly prized a scroll of com-
mendation from General Mark W. Clark, a bronze star, four
battle stars, to say nothing of the Order of the Crown of
Italy for my service as Allied military governor for the province of Reggio nell' Emilia. Really all I wanted was a speedy
return to civilian life.

Cleveland looked beautiful. It is not noted for its glamor,
but it certainly looked marvelous to me. Even more marvelous was the sight of Ruby, who met me at the train.

I wanted to spend a lot of time doing nothing and making
up to Ruby for her years of loneliness, but life has a way
of closing in before you can stop it. I wasn't out of uniform
when I got my first fee as a practising lawyer again. I didn't

even have an office. I found myself defending a man indicted on an income tax violation. Soon afterwards I was involved in another case, a damage suit for personal injury.

As soon as I could extricate myself from business, Ruby and I went on a trip to New Orleans, a kind of second honeymoon. Italy, when I thought of it at all, seemed like a place where I had never been and the war a nightmare from which I had awakened. I had expected the experience of war to harden me. I found that the opposite had happened. But the war had increased the determination I had felt ever since I had seen that man being beaten by a policeman in Ohio when I was a little boy—to fight against injustice. Whatever I did from here on, I wanted to be certain it would be in the cause of justice, in the certainty of human betterment, whether for one man accused of a crime he had not committed, or for millions denied the opportunity to realize their full potential as human beings by the selfish interests of some powerful faction.

When we returned to Cleveland, I opened an office with several other lawyers. I plunged into work. Probably the most famous case I handled was the trial of Thomas Sanfillippo. It was in the fall of 1946. On the evidence of a hat found at the scene of the crime, with markings of a hat cleaner which enabled detectives to trace it to Sanfillippo, and some fragments of glass in his trouser cuff identified by a professor as identical with glass from a Dodge automobile, the prosecuting attorney was trying to send Sanfillippo to the electric chair for the murder of Robert L. Firestone, a Cleveland racketeer. The defendant was a large man with dark hair and a sallow face. Like a movie gangster, he had a scar on the left side of his forehead which, I had a feeling, might tempt the jury to jump to conclusions. He took the stand himself to deny he had been anywhere near the scene of the ambush-slaying and to say that the hat was one he had left several days earlier in a restaurant; we had evidence that the trousers, the cuffs of which contained the particles of glass about which the state's professional witness testified, were at a cleaner's at the time of the slaying. Also I offered expert testimony from the Cleveland weatherman, who testified that the wind velocity was such that had the hat fallen from or blown off the head of a man running from the murder scene, it would have been found yards away from the other side of the victim's automobile instead of where it actually was found. The prosecution's case was that Firestone after closing his night club in Shaker Heights at 3:30 a.m., took a waitress home and that later the Firestone coupe was apparently forced to the curb by men in another automobile. There was an argument between Firestone, seated at the driver's wheel of his coupe, and a man or men standing close by. Firestone died in a hospital a few hours after the shooting without giving the police any information.

One eyewitness, a taxi driver who claimed he had seen Sanfillippo enter a night club after the shooting, was conveniently in Florida. Another eyewitness was reportedly in California.

Another taxi driver, who did testify at the trial, said he had been awakened at his home by the sound of scraping fenders on the night of the murder and had looked out to see three parked automobiles across the street. He claimed he had also seen flashes of gunfire and a man speeding away in a car, but admitted he could not identify the murderer. "There are men," said the county prosecutor, James P. Hart, in his closing argument against Sanfillippo to a jury of ten women and two men, "who need no motive but gold." My colleague, defense attorney Gerard Pilliod, branded the circumstantial evidence—the hat and the grains of glass supposed to have come from Sanfillippo's trouser cuff—as items of "speculation," "drastic inference." I addressed the jury

225

for almost ninety minutes on the ninth day of the trial, picking away piece by piece at the state's case, which was indeed circumstantial.

Mrs. Marge Sanfillippo was every inch a lady. She had married Tom Sanfillippo when she was seventeen years old. They had several children. My associate had nearly persuaded me not to place her in the witness stand. Then, on a Sunday afternoon when the defense was nearing the close of our case, I had Ruby meet Mrs. Sanfillippo. We three talked, and my wife, whose judgment I always found sound, overruled me. She said, "You must place Mrs. Sanfillippo on the witness stand and have her tell her story just as she told it to me. You will lose your case if you don't." I shall never forget the sobs of Marge Sanfillippo when the jury returned with a verdict of not guilty after five hours and thirty-five minutes deliberation. No real motive had been laid at the door of Sanfillippo, no witness had been able to identify him as the man who shot Firestone. All the prosecution's case had centered around that hat found near the scene of the crime. I believe to this day the jurors were right.

Ever since that day in 1946 when Sanfillippo was acquitted, Marjorie Sanfillippo has sent me a Countess Mara tie on Christmas. I still have the first one.

Another spectacular case in which I was involved was the trial of Wallace Lee, a Cleveland Negro who had no previous criminal record at all. Lee had been accused of holding up a cab driver. The cab driver looked at Lee and said he was the man who had put a gun to his head. Lee had a brother who was in Cleveland. After court recess, I had the defendant sit in the first row of spectators. The cab driver didn't point to him when he was asked this time who had held him up. He pointed to Lee's brother. I cross-examined him. If he had pointed to Wallace Lee, plainly visible in the front row, a verdict of guilty would have been returned. But he didn't. I knew the time was right and I said, "Wallace Lee, please stand up." There was what they call in courtroom dramas a sensation and the judge, whose name was Orr and who was trying his first criminal case, got red in the face and granted a mistrial.

Three days later Judge Orr went to the hospital. I don't know whether or not the case put him there.

When Wallace Lee was re-indicted I claimed double jeopardy, but this was turned down. And so, about thirteen months later, once again Wallace Lee was up for trial for the same hold-up of the same cab driver, this time before Judge Frank S. Day.

Judge Day said to me quite calmly, "Is that the defendant sitting behind you?"

I said it was.

"Well," said the Judge, "see that he stays there."

The jury found Lee not guilty.

A television program a few years ago based a complete half-hour story on the case of the State of Ohio vs. Wallace Lee. They made quite a hero of the defense counsel for his stratagem. Maybe I should have sued for damages for invasion of privacy.

Later I heard of a lawyer in some other part of the country who tried the same stratagem. Unfortunately for him, the witness this time pointed correctly at the man for whom the substitution had been made, and the lawyer lost the case.

It took longer to settle down in my private life than in my profession. Ruby and I lived in a hotel room for many months before we finally fixed up an apartment in Shaker Square. Stephen Junior was down in Key West, Florida, doing personnel work. Dick had married a girl from Jackson, Michigan. He was out of the Navy and working in Toledo at a modest job. Later he went back to law school and followed in the family footsteps. I had five grandchildren. My mother was still alive in Norwalk, where I often visited her. She was in her nineties.

227

Although I was making money as a lawyer, leading a more tranquil life than I had ever done in Washington, by 1948 Potomac fever got me again and I decided to run for Congressman-at-large once more. I was nominated and elected without trouble. The only opposition I got was from Ruby. She felt I was doing well enough as a lawyer and ought to stay out of politics.

On New Year's Day, 1949, somewhat weary from seeing the new year in until 5:00 a.m., I got on a train for Washington. I had to be there in time for a Democratic caucus next morning to fill a vacancy on the Ways and Means Committee and to decide on the Speaker, Majority Leader and officers of the House of Representatives. The Committee on Ways and Means is really the only Constitutional committee in either branch of the Congress, and membership is highly coveted.

When I walked into the caucus room Speaker Sam Rayburn said, "Steve, where have you been? We want you to go on Ways and Means."

I said, "Thank you, Mr. Speaker. If you want me, I'll be glad to be a candidate." Since such membership usually goes to members with seniority, of which I had none, I was surprised, but Rayburn managed to scare up a precedent for me —William Jennings Bryan had served without seniority on this very committee. The truth was, both Truman and Rayburn wanted a Northern liberal. A fine conservative Democrat from Virginia, who was later to be Governor of the Old Dominion, if elected to this powerful committee might have thrown the balance against the progressive legislation desired by President Truman. I heard a murmur going around the room: "Rayburn wants Young." Throughout the caucus I sat silent. Most of the Democratic Representatives there were strangers to me. I won by some forty votes.

The Ways and Means Committee is the most powerful

228

committee in the House of Representatives. It has exclusive jurisdiction over all bills relating to money and taxes. There are twenty-five members. The Democratic members of the Ways and Means also select the Democratic members of all other committees.

Those two years in the Eighty-first Congress were a real education. I learned more about the way this government operates than I had during any of my previous terms. I found myself in the center of things. The only trouble was that to serve on the Ways and Means Committee you have to be a mathematician as well as a politician. I don't think I ever learned how to read a budget properly, and at the end of one of those sessions numbers and dollars signs would be swimming before my eyes. But the real work of the Ways and Means Committee is not done in its official sessions. Things actually start to get done when you sit in your shirtsleeves in the evening, talk back and forth and settle questions informally.

Early in March 1949 I spoke at a meeting of the Northern Ohio Industrial Editors Association. I directly assailed Senator Robert A. Taft for his conservative views. Now the fact is Ohio has been not only the cradle of Presidents, but also the cradle of a particularly stubborn and static brand of conservatism. Ohioans are property conscious and, especially, land conscious. Just about every fourth family in Ohio in those days was interested in farming. Now the number has fallen off somewhat but, with one quarter of the population engaged in farming to varying degrees, it is not surprising that the political leanings of so many Ohioans have been more to the right than to the left. Farmers have always been conservative.

Senator Taft was an isolationist. He had opposed all New Deal measures, which he would inevitably term socialistic. He was not for the little man (unless, perhaps, for the little businessman). He was definitely anti-Labor. Yet even Taft's

229

Senate enemies always spoke of him with a certain reverence and respect. He had great industry. He had courage. He was consistent almost on a grand scale. You knew where you stood with him. He was a conservative, but an honest conservative. He would not compromise as a matter of convenience or to advance personal ambitions. He had no confidence in the masses of the people—in that sense I suppose he was a Hamiltonian—but he never said one thing and did another. He was honest.

I had never said much about him before, but at that lunch of the Industrial Editors I really lashed into him. "Last week Robert Alonzo Taft," I said, "came to Cleveland and warned that if President Truman's program is enacted into law by Congress, this nation would fast have complete regimentation, entry of government into business and a greatly increased tax load." I said that when Taft talked of regimentation he was forgetting that the Republicans had regimented the largest army of unemployed the world had ever seen. Republicans like Senator Taft praised rugged individualism, but the last Republican administration produced ragged individuals. I talked against the Taft-Hartley Act. I made note of the fact that the Republican Eightieth Congress had appropriated sixty million dollars for the eradication of hoof and mouth disease in Mexican cattle, reduced the school lunches for needy children and made no provision for public health programs.

In Congress Democrats continued to fight for expanding social security benefits and federal aid for low cost housing. We voted for an act providing permanent price support programs for agricultural commodities; for an act raising the minimum wage from 40 to 75 cents an hour, causing more than a million workers to receive increases; for a three-year extension of the President's authority to enter into trade agreements without hampering restrictions. This restored the foreign trade policies inaugurated by FDR, under which

230

new markets were opened for business in all parts of the world.

We also voted for foreign military assistance to create an effective system of individual and collective self-defense in support of the purposes of the United Nations charter.

Mindful of the dangers of Communism we passed the Internal Security Act of 1950 to protect this country against Communist aggression and subversion; the act provided for the internment of dangerous Reds in time of war, the strengthening of espionage and sabotage laws, the barring of Communists from defense plants, revision of immigration laws and required registration of Communist front organizations. I hardly need stress the later shocking misapplications of some of the provisions of this act.

On the domestic scene, we voted to extend and liberalize social security coverage to approximately ten million additional persons, bringing the total covered to forty-five million.

We also put through increased taxes to deal with Communist aggression in Korea and authorized more than one billion dollars in aid to NATO countries.

Taking part in the war had not altered my opinion about bonuses for veterans. I jeopardized my re-election by standing up against Representative John Rankin, as well as Ohio lobbyists, and calling Rankin's proposals for special benefits for war veterans a raid on the United States Treasury. In debating with him I refrained from saying that both my sons had fought and been wounded in the Pacific, but the Washington *Post* was kind enough to say it for me.

In the Eighty-first Congress I also resumed my career-long battle against sales taxes. I had fought a losing fight against the sales tax in Ohio and I lost again trying to prevent a sales tax in the District of Columbia.

In 1950, not yet over the shock of the Second World War, we were once again confronted with rising threats to the peace of the world. The Cold War had reached the boiling point in the battleground of Korea. Meanwhile, men like Senator Joe McCarthy were preparing to twist our natural suspicions of our enemies into a search under the nation's beds for subversives. Soon the witch-hunting days of Salem would be upon us again.

I spoke up against this early. "This excitement about a few men seeking to overturn the government of the United States—this looking for Communists under every bed—reminds one of the poem:

'I saw last night upon the stair
A little man who wasn't there.
He wasn't there again today
Oh how I wish he'd go away!' "

Actually, during an earlier term of Congress I once had a little spy scare of my own. As far back as 1941 I had suspected my rival, George H. Bender, of some dirty work at the crossroads. Later that year, when it came to my attention that one of the stenographers in my office was on friendly terms with Congressman Bender and members of his staff, I tried to attribute it to the long arm of coincidence and the smallness of the world we live in. Even so, it did seem rather strange that, of all the thousands of stenographers employed in the political offices in Washington, it had to be a member of my staff who was seen going into his office with him and others of his staff on social occasions. My secretary murmured one day of her suspicions. I scoffed at the idea that anyone on my staff, even this recently employed stenographer, would be disloyal and dismissed the whole matter from my mind. Then one day Congressman Bender made a speech in the House of Representatives and followed it with a statement condemning Americans for being ignorant of the great history and noble traditions of our own country, of knowing more about Romulus and Remus than of American heroes such as Davy Crockett. It so happened that I had re-

232

cently completed writing an article on this subject and had done considerable research during the preceding weeks. Congressman Bender's remarks were startlingly familiar to me, even the phrases he used. I called in the young lady. There was no difficulty about removing her from my payroll. She was quite unrepentant. She said, "What I do after hours is my business, and if I want to give Mr. Bender any suggestions or associate with him and those in his office, that's my own business."

George H. Bender died suddenly in 1961. For some years there was bitter feeling between him and me. On one occasion back in 1941, I believe, in the reading room adjacent to the chamber of the House of Representatives, he and I nearly came to blows. Other Congressmen separated us. Time takes care of such matters, however, and in later years we were on friendly terms. In fact, he told me he was one of the few who had sense enough to bet on me to beat Bricker and that he had won plenty. *De mortuis nil nisi bonum*—but Mr. Bender was not the noblest statesman of my acquaintance.

In 1950 I ran for re-election for the fifth time as Congressman-at-large for the state of Ohio. Many of the newspapers who had supported me in the past now turned against me, to my surprise. I remember visiting my mother on a morning when I felt pretty low because the Cleveland *Plain Dealer*, which usually supported me and had in the past editorially praised my industry and record as Congressman-at-large, had just endorsed Mr. Bender.

"Pet," my mother said after greeting me, "I do believe my eyes are failing." She was ninety-three at the time.

"Well," I asked, "when did you have your glasses changed last?"

"Oh, I don't know, but when I read the *Plain Dealer* for half an hour these days I get a headache."

"Mom," I said, "that's nothing. I read the *Plain Dealer* for ten seconds this morning and I got a headache, too."

CHAPTER 17

🖎 *When people ask me why I was defeated in the 1950 election I like to put the blame on Joe Ferguson, who was Robert Taft's Democratic opponent that year. Joe is a good Democrat. He has served as state auditor and state treasurer. He had enthusiastic followers in the Democratic party but very few Republican or independent voters regarded him as Senatorial timber. There were a number of candidates for the Democratic nomination at our primary in 1950, but he won the nomination. Many campaign stories were told about Joe Ferguson. One was that when asked, "What are your views on Formosa?" he is reported to have replied, "Oh, I have always carried Formosa." Perhaps a better reason for my defeat in 1950 was that I had worked hard and constantly in Washington as a member of the Ways and Means Committee and had neglected "to build my fences back home." George Bender was an indefatigable campaigner, he had a big campaign fund and had really spent most of the entire two years following his defeat in 1948 campaigning for re-election. I had expected to win—I lost.*

On January 2, 1951, I decided to call on President Truman to pay my respects before I left for Cleveland. I expected that my secretary would be able to get an appointment from the White House in a couple of weeks, and was planning to return as soon as I heard. Instead, she got a call back about an hour later. The President wanted to see me the following morning.

I kept wondering why Truman could find time to see me so quickly. I imagined perhaps a reprimand for being defeated, for it was common gossip that the plain-talking President did not think much of "lame duck" Democratic Congressmen. I was ushered into the business part of the executive mansion. I decided I had better speak first because it might be my last opportunity to say anything.

"Mr. President," I said, "I'm about to leave for Ohio. Before leaving I wanted to say goodbye to you personally and to tell you that the last two years of service have been the most satisfying of all the times I have been Congressman-at-large from Ohio. I feel I owe the opportunity to learn so much about our government in the past two years to the courageous campaign you made for election."

I was referring to Truman's whistle-stop campaign of 1948. Truman had spoken plain words to the people of America, face to face, in town after town month after month. In the future that will be regarded in American political annals as the most courageous campaign ever undertaken by a Presidential candidate.

I told the President, "In the main I have supported you and your program and I'm only regretful I won't have the chance to be here to give you further support during the next two years." Then I found out why the President had responded so promptly to my request to see him.

"Steve," he said, "how would you like to be United States judge for the Northern District of Ohio?"

"I would like that very much, Mr. President," I managed to say, "but I didn't intend to talk with you about that."

"I know that," he said, "but let the record show I brought it up." He explained that his question about the judgeship could not be considered a definite commitment because there were some "hurdles" we would have to overcome before I

236

could be appointed. "Yes," I replied, "I know two of them. One is named Taft and the other is named Bricker."

We agreed that perhaps these hurdles could be overcome. I repeated that I had not expected the offer to be made, adding, "I will certainly be elated if such an appointment comes my way."

"I am glad to hear that, Steve," Truman said. "It will come your way."

I was happy when I walked out of the White House. Almost immediately I called Ruby to tell her.

"Don't count on it," was her reaction. "We've met with a lot of disappointments, you know."

Even so, it took a little while for me to calm down sufficiently to plan my strategy. I urged friends to write the two Senators from Ohio, informing them that the President was considering me for the opening. Pretty soon reports began to trickle back, mainly from newspapermen. The first was from Senator Taft, who had stated, "I don't know Steve Young personally too well, but I have met him a few times. I know he is a man of great industry. I will not object to his appointment."

Later I was told that Senator Bricker had said, "Oh, Steve? Yes, he's all right and his wife is a good friend of my wife. If his name comes before me I won't object."

If a Senator from your home state *does* object to your appointment as a judge, you might just as well forget about it. Knowing that Senators Taft and Bricker were raising no obstacles, I felt considerably heartened.

Difficulties soon arose from another direction. Cleveland newspapers published the fact that the FBI was investigating me in connection with the pending vacancy for United States District Judge. Investigation by the FBI is invariably the last step before the nomination is announced from the White House. Immediately following the publication, Democratic county chairman Ray T. Miller, Cleveland Mayor Thomas

A. Burke and other Democratic organization political leaders from Cleveland zeroed in on Washington. Some were friends of Attorney General McGrath and opposed to my appointment; they urged the appointment of Don C. Miller, United States Attorney and a brother of county chairman Ray T. Miller. Don Miller, who in my opinion is a competent lawyer and a personable, fine man, was generally regarded as the leading candidate for appointment to the vacant judgeship. The fact that his brother Ray was then Democratic chairman of Cuyahoga County boded well for his chances and ill for mine.

When Mayor Tom Burke and Democratic chairman Miller finished denouncing me to Attorney General McGrath and at the White House, my budding judicial career had withered. Don Miller, I am sorry to say, did not receive the appointment. Congressman Crosser recommended a Cleveland judge who later was appointed. In 1960, after Claiborne Pell beat Harold McGrath for the Democratic nomination for United States Senator from Rhode Island, I took pleasure in thanking McGrath for his recommendation against me; without it I would not be a Senator today.

I learned from a reliable source in Cleveland that the FBI report about me was good. The only questionable or objectionable feature in it was a statement that "his son, Stephen Junior was a member of the Abraham Lincoln Brigade." Let us hope that FBI reports are generally more reliable than this.

I was reminded by my wife, Ruby, that during my second term as Congressman-at-large Governor George White's son had, according to newspaper accounts, enlisted in the Abraham Lincoln Brigade while a senior at Princeton. It was kind of fashionable in the mid-thirties to do so. Apparently our son, Stephen Junior following a college fraternity party, said he was going to enlist to fight in the Spanish Civil War. He never did. He had never seen Spain, but the FBI reported he had joined the Brigade.

238

Probably it was as well I wasn't appointed. I had never been a good organization Democrat and I was always too much of a partisan lawyer to feel right on the bench. I had been used to seeing one side of a question. Nor do I think a man should ever serve as a judge unless he wants to make a lifetime career of it.

From the time of my defeat for re-election as Congressman-at-large in 1950 to the day I was sworn in as United States Senator I never came back to Capitol Hill—except once. That was the day I appeared as president of the Cuyahoga County Bar Association before the Senate Finance Committee in 1956 to urge that lawyers be included under social security coverage. (As a matter of fact, I was the first president of any bar association to do so.)

It is my observation as a Congressman that once you're out, you're out. When I returned to my Cleveland law practice I hoped to be considered as counsel for the Ways and Means Committee. I wrote a letter to Congressman Cecil King of California. We had served together on the Ways and Means Committee and had been good friends. I said I was not interested in what my salary would be or whether I got any remuneration at all. I said I was willing to devote practically all my time, if that was necessary, to such duties as I would have as counsel to the committee while Congress was in session. I never even received an answer. When I was a Congressman I remember getting into an elevator just as an ex-Congressman was leaving. One of the men with me said, "I wonder how the poor old guy is getting along." It might well be he was getting along very well indeed, but some Congressmen seem to feel rather smug.

The early 1950's were good years in America—a kind of hiatus between crises, an era of brief respite, of expectation that the UN would before long solve all the world's problems in good faith—then the Korean episode brought bloodshed again. They were good years for me, too, as far as my career as a lawyer was concerned.

They were also years of personal heartbreak. In 1950 my wife became seriously ill. In the spring of 1952 our doctor told me she would not live more than six months. She had been operated on in 1948 for cancer of the breast. Now she had cancer of the lung. On October 30, 1952, she died. I began to feel guilty because I hadn't told her that her illness was fatal, although I believe she did know it. I think many men will say, without question, that their wives are invariably smarter than they are. A year earlier I had lost my mother. She had died in Norwalk at the age of ninety-four; until the end she had all her faculties. Following the death of my wife, I took some night courses at Western Reserve University to keep me busy. One course I recommend to anyone was a rapid reading course; later, as Senator, along with Edward Kennedy, Dan Inouye and others I took a refresher course in rapid reading.

These personal tragedies caused me more than ever to turn my attention and my energies to my practice. Business boomed and my election as president of the Cuyahoga Bar Association in the spring of 1953 did not hurt.

I headed a vigorous drive against those posing as working lawyers without proper authority and credentials. I urged less emphasis on pre-trial hearings. I headed a campaign to investigate charges of police brutality which came to light in the case of Louis Varro, who was accused of bank robbery and had his nose broken during questioning by police. I encouraged the organization of the Cleveland Lawyers Reference Plan which enabled those in need of legal advice to consult an attorney for an initial consultation fee of only five dollars. The Cuyahoga Bar Association to this day maintains this reference bureau and frequently advertises the service in Cleveland newspapers. I also interested myself in a crusade against bar association restrictions on the press in court cases.

240

In 1956 I was once more tempted into the political arena, this time as candidate for attorney general of Ohio. (I had run for this office before, in 1922.) I had the bad judgment to choose the year when Dwight D. Eisenhower was running for the Presidency. It was, to put it mildly, a Republican year.

During the fifties I also became involved in an organization known as the Council on World Affairs, a bipartisan group of Clevelanders with an active interest in a program designed to create interest in America's involvement in the destiny of all nations. We were able to get together some prominent speakers. I also worked in Good Will Industries, an organization which helps handicapped people to do useful work.

I don't mean to convey the impression that I spent all my time being a "do-gooder." Ruby's death had left a terrible void in my life, a void that time and activities helped to fill, but with little success, until I met Rachel in Florida in 1956.

Rachel and I made several trips to Italy. With all the rebuilding that had been done, I could hardly believe it was the same country I had known during the Second World War. Walking through the streets of Florence I remembered the street fighting that had taken place there. How different it all looked on a quiet weekend in the summer of 1957, my wife at my side!

I was enjoying my work as a lawyer, my local fame and even occasional notoriety. I had good friends and a wonderful family. I might have lived out my life without ever again seeing Washington or setting foot again in the halls of Congress.

But in 1958 because the thought of Ohio represented for another term by Senator Bricker filled me with an unutterable gloom, I resolved to run against him. I was sixty-eight.

CHAPTER 18

✍ *A fellow once asked me, "Senator, after all these years in Congress, if you had the power to completely reshape our federal legislative bodies, how would you change them?"*

The answer is, not too much. I certainly would like to see some aspects of Congress improved, but I think our founding fathers planned better than they knew when they separated the legislative, judicial and executive branches of our government and divided Congress into two houses. I rather cherish the symbolism of the White House being a full mile from the Capitol, and I think, by and large, the machinery of Congress is organized sensibly.

I would favor streamlining the House of Representatives. It is too crowded today to run smoothly. I think its business could be conducted more efficiently if there were apportionment on the basis of one Representative to every 800,000 or million citizens in a district. Today there is one Representative for every 450,000. I think the body could be made up of one-third of the present representation.

I would also take away from the Rules Committee the right to throttle legislation.

I would like to see a procedure established whereby a Senator's remarks or material could be directly entered into the *Congressional Record.* Having to cover every time with a spoken preamble on the Senate floor seems an absurd waste of time. Anyone who has sat in the House or Senate listening to one Senator or Representative talking, as it were, to himself in order to have his remarks part of the *Record* would agree, I think.

I would also like to see the actual Congressional session shortened. Under our Constitution both Houses are, in theory, equal. Neither body can recess for more than three days without the consent of the other.

I think Congress ought to be divided into two sessions so that all members can get home for at least thirty days between sessions to meet with the citizens who have elected them, report to them and get to know at firsthand what their wishes are. Perhaps the first session of Congress might consider only money bills—the budget, for example. That might take until June. After the thirty-day recess the second session could consider bills other than those concerned with finances.

I should also like to see joint sessions held frequently by important committees. I would suggest that the chairman of the House committee and the chairman of the Senate committee preside alternately at these joint meetings. Today, for example, the Secretaries of Defense, Army, Navy and Air Force must testify separately before each committee. Why not testify before both simultaneously? It would certainly save time.

I think it might also be helpful if two days of the week, when neither the Senate nor the House would be in session, were set aside for committee meetings. Even when these bodies are not in session I would still like to see days set aside for the committees to meet. Then when they did meet it would be possible to discuss issues more fully.

I have always been opposed to limiting debate in the Senate, but I believe it might be a good idea to be able to limit debate by a vote of three-fifths instead of by two-thirds of Senators present and voting.

In the light (or perhaps I should say the darkness) of the recent scandals, I have also come to believe strongly that it would be a good idea to adopt a rule about the value of gifts a Senator or Representative may accept. Senator Paul Douglas refuses to accept any gift worth more than two and a half dollars. I think I would set the limit at five dollars; a good fifth of bourbon costs more than two and a half. In the White House under President Kennedy two employees worked full-time appraising, rewrapping and sending back any gifts worth more than fifteen dollars. It is not that I think the country is tottering because the President gets a phonograph or the wife of the Chief Justice is offered a deep-freeze, or because General Eisenhower, while President, received more than fifty thousand dollars' worth of gifts for his Gettysburg farm. I just think it's unbecoming for the nation's leaders to accept valuable gifts or to be put in the position of being subject to possible bribes or temptations.

Clearly, my thoughts on the subject of reshaping Congress are far from revolutionary. If we elect the best possible men, the pattern is viable and democratic. On the other hand, I am beginning to think it is time we held another Constitutional Convention as provided for by our forebears.

This nation began as a country peopled by three million frontier farmers with a sprinkling of merchants, importers and men in the fishing industry. Since then our Constitution has been amended twenty-four times. If George Washington and Benjamin Franklin came back today, they wouldn't know their own country. Yet we still wear the same political cloak. Forty men devised our Constitution, most of them lawyers. They were the conservatives of their day. Franklin's suggestion that each day's session be opened with a prayer didn't receive even one supporting vote. I think, considering the size of our country now, the technological changes that have swept our world, the enormous responsibilities that devolve on the federal government, that the Constitution with all its amendments has become something of a patchwork. I believe it could be revised to the advantage of all. I would not change the first ten amendments—our Bill of Rights, which enables us to breathe as free men. But there are other changes which could improve the original document. Such a convention might determine, for example, that the Senate be composed not of two Senators from every state of the union, but that there be at least one more Senator from each state in proportion to state population. We might have a body of 120 or 130 Senators instead of the hundred we have now, but representation might be more fair.

I can also imagine such a convention changing the laws to give the country two Vice-Presidents. Indeed, in 1963, shortly after the assassination of President Kennedy, I introduced an alternative step—a resolution calling for a constitutional amendment which would provide, in the event the office of Vice-President becomes vacant, for the President to nominate a new Vice-President within sixty days, subject to confirmation by the Senate. Such a procedure would assure continuity of party and policy. The new Vice-President could quickly be confirmed by majority vote of the Senate and the leadership of the country made that much more secure.

The more I reflect on these questions of possible change, however, the more I am impressed not so much with the weaknesses of our system as with its strength and vitality. Again and again we have proved that our flexible and representative form of government is equal to all the changing weathers of political events. Unlike so many governments in this perilous world, we stand firm through every crisis. When President Kennedy was assassinated on November 22, 1963, I happened to be at my desk in the Senate chamber. The Senate was debating a library bill. There were about twenty Senators in the chamber. I was about to go out into the corridor or perhaps into the reading room until something interesting came up when an assistant sergeant-at-arms came over to tell me the President had been shot. I said, "Oh, no!" I was stunned. All of us were. I remember starting forward to tell the President's brother, Senator Edward Kennedy, who was presiding at the time. Senator Holland of Florida had already reached him. I went into the corridor to stand at the news ticker, a dazed man in a dazed crowd. When the report came in, "The President is dead," who could believe it? Our forty-six-year-old Chief Executive, a happy husband, father of two small children, brilliant, eager, foremost leader of the free world, would no longer direct the destiny of freedom-loving people the world over. In World War II his life was saved in enemy action. Now he had lost his life. How could be be replaced? Would not the reins that held the world from plunging into insanity go slack? Would not our enemies take advantage of our grief and confusion to strike against us? A little later we heard the voice of President Johnson. We closed ranks in spiritual solidarity. President Johnson's first address to Congress—in reality to the nation—reflected his intent to carry forward the programs of his predecessor. We are not plunged into panic or confusion or civil war. Once again our form of government had stood the test of crisis. We came through. We had lost a great leader. We had not lost our continuity as a strong, sane people.

We often laugh at our leaders, and that is healthy. There is perhaps no body more vulnerable than Congress to the gibes and lampoons of the satirist. That, too, is healthy. But beneath the laughter is loyalty, the knowledge of every sane American that democracy is still the last, best hope of earth.

During my term as Senator a number of men dear to me have died; not only our President, from whom we who loved him expected so much, but many of my colleagues in the Senate as well. There was William Langer of North Dakota, always a valiant battler for the underdog and politically independent, who overcame great obstacles in his long life; Richard

247

Neuberger of Oregon, a man of great intellect and humanity who died March 9, 1960; Thomas C. Hennings of Missouri who died in 1960, a personal friend from my years in the House of Representatives, a champion of freedom of speech, immune throughout the McCarthy era to the witch-hunting virus that infected so many others; Francis Case of South Dakota, a hard-working and scrupulous man who died in 1962; Dennis Chavez of New Mexico, a fighter for the rights of the underdog all his life in the House and later in the Senate, also dead in 1962; Robert S. Kerr of Oklahoma, a marvelous spellbinder whom I often voted against but whom I respected and liked, who died in 1963. Also in 1963 we lost Estes Kefauver, a man who seemed mild but was totally fearless when it came to combating crime and dishonesty; a wonderful crusader, an irreplaceable man who, in my opinion, would have made a good President.

We have lost some great leaders, but the Senate remains a place of tremendous vitality. It was originally conceived as a body of elder statesmen who, by their sagacity and conservatism, would restrain the radical impetuosity of youth more prevalent in the House. The picture is quite different today. It is in the Senate that one finds progressive thought, the courage to change the old, to go forward, although there always seems to be a "little group of willful men" to obstruct legislation such as the civil rights bill. In the end, however, sanity nearly always triumphs on the Senate floor. The really conservative body today, where most of the muddled thinking is done and the brakes are too frequently put on progress, is the House of Representatives.

Recently a young man came to me and asked me if he ought to go into politics. Since he was an intelligent chap with a pleasing personality and considerable talent and abilty, I advised him heartily to do so, for I think politics remains one of the most effective and meaningful careers anyone can choose. I suggested that he move into a community

248

away from the place where he was born and raised, join the church of his choice, the party of his choice, work as a precinct committeeman and study our country's political history, the problems and conflicts which have faced us and how we have solved them. I advised him that he should not feel above menial work for the party organization. I advised him to be patient, to acquire political skill, rather than to get elected first and try to learn statesmanship later. I also advised him to develop a strong stomach for chicken dinners, cocktail parties, oratory and television make-up men. I did not say anything about kissing babies or wearing big hats or knuckling under to party bosses; the image of the politician as a hearty, bluff extrovert with a big mouth and big handshake is due for the scrap heap. A young man today (or any day), whether planning to enter politics or any other field of endeavor, should learn to adhere to his own beliefs no matter how unpopular they are. Being a good actor may be an asset, but being honest is essential. There is no substitute.

When I look back on the long years of my own career in politics, I realize how great a teacher time is. I think I am only now beginning to learn what I thought I knew so well when I was thirty. I hope in future years I can live up to the advice offered by T. S. Eliot: old men should be explorers. Of course, by Senatorial standards, a man of my age hardly qualifies as old these days. Carl Hayden, our oldest Senator, is eighty-six and can remember being a sheriff in his state of Arizona when it was still a territory. The youngest is Edward Kennedy, a chap I have come to admire increasingly ever since his election; he is piling up a fine record.

We live in a time when the greatest threat is to the individuality and the humanity of a man. Automation does not only threaten his job, even while it provides him with new conveniences and comforts; it also threatens to make him a faceless cipher, a number, a card in an IBM index; an undistinguished, indistinguishable duplicate of his neighbor. Only education can combat this, education which equips men to learn to know themselves, to recognize the truth and to realize the full promise and potential of their inheritance.

If politicians will but behave as statesmen, America may well lead the way toward this enlightenment. There were many times in my life when I was making a comfortable living as a lawyer and could have pleased those who loved me most dearly by remaining away from the political arena and being content with a less strenuous career. It is true enough that politics is a virus and that, once you're bitten, recovery is difficult, and true enough that the attention a Congressman receives is gratifying to the child in him and the hungry ego. Yet it is also true that there is no satisfaction like that of knowing your day's work has been of a significance to the welfare of your fellow men on a scale only possible in the national and international arena of political life. Perhaps that is why Pericles remarked thousands of years ago: "We do not say that a man who takes no interest in politics minds his own business. We say he has no business here at all."

POSTSCRIPT

Early in May 1963, long before I had announced my own decision to run again for the Senate, rumors began to reach me of a threat to my candidacy that seemed in more ways than one to be coming at me right out of the blue. Lieutenant Colonel John Glenn of the United States Marine Corps, the first American to orbit the earth, was reported to have his eye on my job. The signals were quite weak and indistinct at first. No one even seemed to be certain whether Lieutenant Colonel Glenn was a Republican or a Democrat. Efforts to pin down this information were unsuccessful, for the colonel continued to describe himself as an independent. On one occasion after "shopping around," talking with Democratic leaders and then later with the Republican National Chairman and with Ray Bliss, Republican State Chairman for Ohio, he had said he considered himself "an independent, but if I have to choose a political party I would regard myself as a moderate Republican or a conservative Democrat."

Then, on January 17, 1964, the colonel announced that he would be a candidate for the Ohio Democratic nomination for United States Senator in the May 5th primary. This announcement promptly catapulted both the colonel and me into the nation's headlines and onto its television screens.

As a member of the Aeronautical and Space Sciences Committee I had voted for the appropriations which made Glenn's achievement possible. More than seven million dol-

251

lars of taxpayers' money was spent to train the seven original astronauts. I remember that when the White House called and told me that one of the seven astronauts was going to be Glenn from my home state, I was jubilant. The fact is, Lt. Col. Glenn is a fine young man, a real hero. He has shown his courage in the ordeal which brought him national acclaim; he has a wonderful personality, a keen mind, humor and charm. Admiring him as an outstanding Ohioan and a national hero, I made up my mind from the first that I would not stoop to *ad hominem* argument in campaigning against him but would confine myself solely to the issues.

In the weeks that followed the way proved murky; nobody seemed able to find out from the colonel where he stood politically. He told the world's press that, as a member of the Marine Corps, he was not permitted to discuss politics until he was mustered out. A reporter for *The Nation*, echoing the questions being asked by journalists throughout the country inquired, "Where does he stand on civil rights? On the tax cut? On federal aid to education? On Medicare? On foreign aid? On Cuba? On Panama? On the sale of wheat to Russia? On a hundred other issues and problems that face legislators? No one but Glenn knows at the moment—if he knows." In its "Notes and Comments" department, the *New Yorker* magazine went so far as to suggest that if the colonel was qualified to run for the Senate, he could have no real objection if I were to "step in to fill the gap left in the astronaut team." I nearly thought that had happened when I picked up the New York *Times* on April 14, 1964 and saw a front-page headline, which read: GRISSOM AND YOUNG WILL BE FIRST CREW FOR A GEMINI FLIGHT. To my relief, when I read further I found they were referring to Lieutenant Commander John W. Young, who isn't even a relative. Better him than me!

Meanwhile, Ed Sullivan reported in his *Daily News* column that Broadway bookies were taking bets favoring astronaut John Glenn seven to five. The cartoonist Herblock, in the Washington *Post*, showed a politician marching with a placard favoring Glenn for United States Senator, while other citizens carried signs calling on everyone from Mickey Mantle to Carol Channing to run for the Senate. And indeed, Coach Bud Wilkinson of the University of Oklahoma, fresh from the gridiron, had tossed his hat into the Senatorial ring.

I tried to force the issue at the unofficial Democratic pre-primary convention, so called, in Columbus. This meeting was held on January 20th, but ended inconclusively with no endorsement for either Glenn or myself.

I was just beginning to enjoy the whole fracas immensely and was looking forward with relish to my opponent's emergence from the Marine Corps' vales of silence into the open arena of political debate when, on February 26th, he suffered a brain concussion and an injury to his inner ear in a bathroom accident. My pleasurable anticipation of a spirited campaign and renomination by a substantial margin vanished and I joined in the national concern for his health.

On March 30th, because of his slow recovery, the lieutenant colonel who had spun about the earth three times and had flown through two wars without a scratch announced his withdrawal from the campaign. Colonel Glenn said he did not think it fair to ask the people of Ohio "to vote for a name." He stated clearly and honestly what had been my own feeling for some time: "No man has a right to ask for a seat in either branch of the Congress merely because of a specific event such as orbiting the earth in a space craft, any more than he would have that right by just being a lawyer and having tried a few cases at the local courthouse." Anyone who can make a statement as outspoken and level-headed as that is going to make a place for himself somewhere in our national life, and I predict a great future for this bright and brave young man.

At the same time I think he was wrong, as I think others

have been wrong who have sought to enter politics from the top. I started running for office fifty-two years ago, ten years before John Glenn was born. Although I have violated all the conventional rules—I am not a diplomat and don't pretend to be; I have always kept my eyes on the nation's welfare instead of on the partisan whims of pressure groups; and, to paraphrase Henry Clay, I would rather be right than Senator—I do believe that a legislator must learn his business from the bottom. Politics is as much a profession as the law or medicine or military science. It calls for training and, above all, it calls for that indispensable first-hand experience which can be acquired only on the slow, hard climb up through the ranks.

That is the path I followed, and however tough the climb may have been at times, it has never been dull. From where I stand now the view is glorious.